LISBON IN THE RENAISSANCE

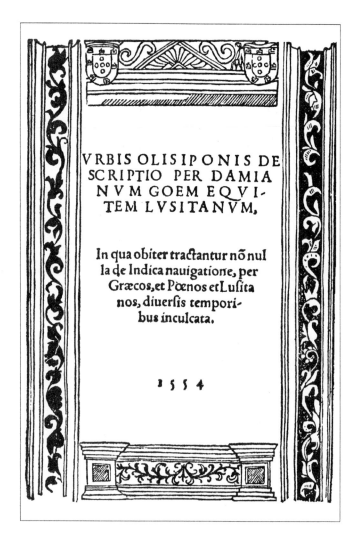

VRBIS OLISIPONIS DE
SCRIPTIO PER DAMIA
NVM GOEM EQVI-
TEM LVSITANVM,

In qua obiter tractantur nõ nul
la de Indica nauigatione, per
Græcos,et Pœnos etLuſita
nos, diuerſis tempori-
bus inculcata.

1554

Damião de Góis

Lisbon in the Renaissance

A NEW TRANSLATION OF THE
URBIS OLISIPONIS DESCRIPTIO
BY
JEFFREY S. RUTH

ITALICA PRESS
NEW YORK
1996

Copyright © 1996 by Jeffrey S. Ruth

ITALICA PRESS, INC.
595 Main Street
New York, New York 10044

Library of Congress Cataloging-in-Publication Data

Góis, Damião de, 1502-1574.
   [Urbis Olisiponis descriptio. English]
   Lisbon in the Renaissance : a new translation of the Urbis Olisiponis descriptio / by Jeffrey S. Ruth.
     p.   cm.
   Includes bibliographical references (p.   ) and index.
   "A translation of the Portuguese version of the Latin text Urbis Olisiponis descriptio"—Preface.
   ISBN 0-934977-36-4 (alk. paper)
   1. Lisbon (Portugal)—Description and travel—Early works to 1800. 2. Lisbon (Portugal)—History. I. Ruth, Jeffrey S., 1959-. II. Title.
   DP756.G68 1996
   946.9'425—dc20
                                96-25081
                                    CIP

Printed in the United States of America
5 4 3

Cover Illustration: Panoramic view of Lisbon, from Georg Braun and Frans Hogenberg, *Civitates orbis terrarum*, vol. 5 (Cologne: Georg Braun, 1598).

To My Parents

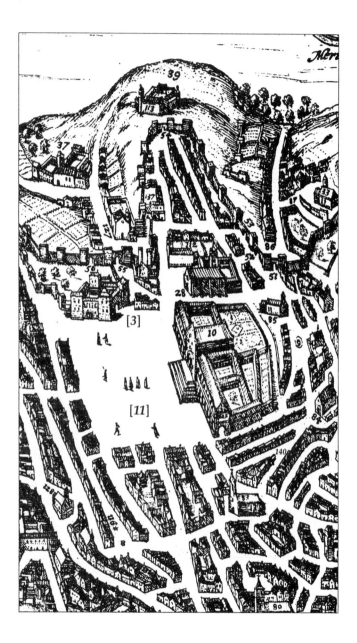

CONTENTS

ILLUSTRATIONS

PREFACE

THIS BOOK OFFERS English-language readers an eye-witness account of Lisbon as a sixteenth-century world capital. It is a translation of the Portuguese version of the Latin text *Urbis Olisiponis Descriptio*, written in 1554 by Portugal's foremost humanist, Damião de Góis. Góis presents his historical and geographical survey of Lisbon in a style meant to emulate that of his humanist peers, including his friend Erasmus of Rotterdam. This description of Lisbon reviews the city's ancient, medieval, and Renaissance history, calling forth the testimony of revered authors to persuade the reader of the city's greatness. The reader is then led through the countryside surrounding Lisbon, and finally to the city center, where attention is called to the chief architectural attractions, to the abundance and wealth of markets, shops, the port district, palaces, and the arsenal. Góis' intent was to prove to his sixteenth-century reader that Portugal's maritime prowess had created in Lisbon a level of power and opulence unrivaled by any city, with the exception of Seville, the major port of Spain's colonial empire. Both cities are called "Queens of the Oceans."

After the lifetime of Damião de Góis, Portugal drifted into a long period of relative decline. In our own times, however, Portugal has once again become very active within the international community, and it seems fitting that a text that so vividly describes Lisbon's past be brought forth now in English translation. *Lisbon in the Renaissance* may be of interest to a great variety of readers, including teachers and students of Portugal, Spain and their former colonial territories; specialists in urban history and in

IX

medieval and Renaissance studies; historians of architecture and of cartography; and travelers, to whom Góis first addressed his book.

This translation is preceded by an introduction and followed by extensive notes, appendices (Chronology of Portugal from the 13th Century, Portuguese Monarchs, Classical Authors Cited), and a three-part bibliography. In addition, the famous Braun and Hogenberg map of Lisbon (from 1598) is reproduced, and keyed to the many streets and buildings visited by Góis in his tour narrative. In choosing the form for names of sites discussed in the text and notes I have most often depended on the context and the survival of these sites with their Portuguese names to the present.

Much of this book was completed in Lisbon during 1989-90, thanks to a generous Fulbright-Hayes research grant. I thank the attentive and friendly staff of the Comissão Cultural Luso-Americana in Lisbon – especially Medith Galvão – for helping me find my way into research collections throughout Lisbon and Portugal, and for easing every step of the project there. José da Felicidade Alves, of the publisher Livros Horizonte, provided me with brief but valuable guidance toward understanding more completely his Portuguese translation of Góis' *Urbis Olisiponis Descriptio*. José Meco's expertise in Portuguese architecture and tiles – offered so generously – sharpened my eye and ultimately brought me a finer appreciation for the details described by Góis. Gina Baptista, dedicated history teacher and immediate friend, inspired me with her own very deep affection for Lisbon's living past. She was unwittingly responsible for my decision to focus on the history of Lisbon while living there, and I thank her for that. Prof. Lydia Hunt of the Monterey Institute of International Studies has my thanks, as well, for her friendship, enthusiasm and guidance on a number of issues in translation. At New York University I received the benefit of generous, critical support in different ways from Professors Helene Anderson, R. Anthony Castagnaro, and Haydee Vitale. All are committed teachers whose perspectives have broadened mine. The unusual contributions of my colleagues in Lisbon – Prof. Francisco Fontes de Sousa (University of Massachusetts, North Dartmouth), Michael Nicklas and Patrick Boland – would be hard to describe and certainly difficult to exaggerate.

Since returning to the United States I have been lucky to have the rare friendship and encouragement of Buddy Garfinkle and Phil Kay. Siglinda Scarpa has been a constant inspiration. Michael Feldstein cared enough to nudge me toward finding a publisher, and then shared in the unfolding of the book. I thank him and other colleagues at The Hudson School – especially Suellen Newman – for their support. At the New York Public Library, Alice Hudson was extremely helpful in locating key maps of Lisbon and Portugal. The James Ford Bell Library at the University of Minnesota kindly provided reproductions from its first edition copy of Góis' text. Its title page is included here. All of the individuals and institutions named above helped make this book better than it would have been without them. They are in no way responsible for any of its shortcomings.

Finally, I thank my family for their support and interest in the development of this book, and most especially Steve and Diana Ruth, for a great deal more than I can express here.

Jeffrey S. Ruth
Hoboken, New Jersey
May 1996

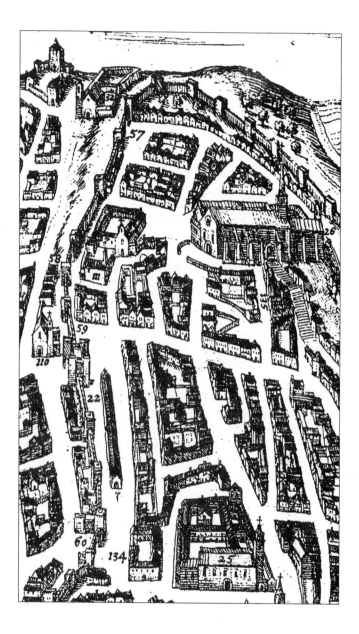

INTRODUCTION

THE AUTHOR

Damião de Góis was born in 1502 to a family of nobles in Alenquer, a town thirty miles north of Lisbon. Góis' life would span the first three-quarters of the sixteenth century, accompanying the exceptionally swift boom-to-bust period of the early Portuguese empire. In his many roles – financial secretary, diplomat, scholar, historian, correspondent and composer – Góis was an active participant in two of Europe's major social convulsions of that time, the Counter Reformation and the expansion of Spain and Portugal into mercantile, colonial powers. Although he lived much of his life as an expatriate in Flanders and traveled widely in Europe, Góis' first and final years were spent in and around Lisbon. The vitality of that city during his lifetime inspired him in 1554 to write *Urbis Olisiponis Descriptio*.[1]

EARLY YEARS

By the age of nine, Damião de Góis had begun his formal education at the court of King Manuel I, in Lisbon. For the following twelve years he had frequent contact with both the tremendous riches imported from Portugal's outposts in Asia, Africa, and America, and also with the foremost intellectual figures of the Manueline court – the playwright Gil Vicente,[2] the mathematician and astronomer Pedro Nunes, the future historian João de Barros, Italian scholars of Latin and Greek, and others. Schooled in languages, sciences, music, and dance, Góis was clearly marked by the secular and innovative spirit that dominated this court, in itself a manifestation of the great national confidence enjoyed in Portugal at the time.

Góis' first patron, King Manuel, oversaw a period of territorial expansion unequaled by Portugal at any time before his reign (1495-1521). Yet Manuel was very much the heir to a nation on the rise. Prior to his accession, the previous monarchs had helped finance annual voyages of exploration since 1415, when Prince Henry ("the Navigator") established a navigational center on the far southwestern cape of Sagres. Together with ongoing crusading expeditions into Morocco, these voyages helped project the power of an ever more knowledgeable Portuguese navy beyond the Iberian Peninsula.

In the 1440s the uninhabited Azore Islands were discovered one thousand miles west in the Atlantic, with settlement promptly following. Off the African coast, the Madeira and Cape Verde island groups were taken, and successive voyages along the coast led Portuguese sailors further south, into the once-feared equatorial latitudes. Fortified trading posts, or *feitorias*, were built along the way, establishing a model for expansion that would become the standard as Portuguese caravels and carracks came to dominate not only the African coasts but those of India and the Moluccas, or Spice, Islands, as well.[3] The Portuguese gained access to these trading routes by first destroying the existing network of Arab merchants in the Indian Ocean that had supplied Europe with Eastern goods into the fifteenth century.[4] With only minimal settlement at each *feitoria*, a flood of wealth and exotica was returned to Lisbon: cinnamon, cloves, nutmeg, mace, ginger, gold, pearls, precious stones, and even elephants. Much of this early success was facilitated by another extremely lucrative new enterprise, that of slave trafficking.[5]

In 1500, while the Spaniards were engaged in vanquishing the inhabitants of their new Caribbean domains, a Portuguese expedition bound for India was blown far to the west, raising land finally upon a coast unknown to them, their future colony of Brazil.[6] Following several decades of relative neglect, by the mid-sixteenth century Brazilian dyewood – *pau brasil* – and sugarcane came to be principal exports to Portugal. Both were produced with African slave labor.

As Damião de Góis entered his teens he frequented the chaotic docks where returning expeditions were received. Later he would vividly recall the sights and sounds of this commercial bustle, the warehouses, armories, a visiting Ethiopian diplomat, the fishmongers, and the great stir caused by Indian elephants and a rhinoceros as they were paraded through the streets of Lisbon. It seems plausible that these experiences, combined with a broad education at the court of Manuel, allowed him to accept with some ease the intriguing new intellectual and social values he later came to know in northern Europe as an adult.

INTELLECTUAL AND PROFESSIONAL GROWTH

In 1521 King Manuel died, and upon his successor and son, João III, fell the obligation of further consolidating the administration of Portugal's new overseas wealth. As a youth of great promise, twenty-one-year-old Damião de Góis was dispatched by João to Antwerp, where for five years he would exercise the office of secretary at the Casa da India, the principal commercial depot in the entire Portuguese empire. Goods from as far away as Macao, off the China coast, and Japan arrived first in Lisbon for registration, but were then transshipped to Antwerp. Ironically, Portugal's poverty prevented the consumption of these exotic cargoes at home, and it was in the port of Antwerp that these riches found distribution into the markets of northern Europe. King Manuel had freely indulged in the capital and expertise of Genovese, Florentine, and German bankers to finance his empire's growth, and these banking families (many of whom also had offices in Antwerp) benefited tremendously from the Portuguese enterprise. Góis lived in Antwerp at a time when that city was the single most vital port in all of northern Europe. As such it not only provided him with great professional challenges, which he executed skillfully,[7] but also thrust him into the acquaintance of newly-reformed Christians, followers of Martin Luther who had made their way into Flanders. Though a Catholic by upbringing, Góis clearly enjoyed the more open social and intellectual life in Antwerp. That city was governed by Charles V, Hapsburg monarch of the Holy Roman Empire and ruler of Spain. Góis found it possible to support him without apparently compromising his allegiance to Portugal, nor his growing interest in the competing Protestant religions.

By 1528 Góis had gained sufficient favor with his king to merit a diplomatic assignment to England, the first of several missions abroad. On the eve of Henry VIII's defection from the Vatican, Góis reassured that monarch of continuing friendship from the Portuguese, not in the least because of their dependence upon trouble-free use of the English Channel for goods bound north to Antwerp.[8] It is likely that Góis met Thomas More at this time, or possibly later in Flanders. Both men were to suffer convictions as heretical Catholics, More for being too dogmatic in Henry's newly-Protestant state, and Góis for being too liberal before the stern eyes of Portugal's Inquisition.

In 1529 Góis traveled to Vilnius (then of Poland) in an unsuccessful effort to arrange for a dynastic marriage between a Portuguese prince, Luis, and a Polish princess, Hedwig. Again in 1531 he traveled to Poland and Russia on a mission of diplomacy, passing en route through Schleswig, Denmark. There he dined with Protestants who, he would later recall to the Inquisition, made a mockery of Catholic rites. (We cannot be sure of Góis' personal reaction.) Then, in Wittenberg, Góis attended a sermon by Martin Luther, whom he considered something of an extremist. Later the two dined, joined by another Lutheran leader, Melancthon, with whom Góis would correspond for seven years. After completing his mission in Russia, and before returning to Flanders, Góis embarked on a voyage along the Don River to visit the Tatar people. This dangerous and purely voluntary excursion to a people feared by most Europeans of his time reflects Góis' anthropological bent. He would later write objectively of these people, as well as of the Lapps he had known in Sweden, and of the Ethiopians he met while in the Manueline court. His curiosity of diverse peoples, and relative respect for them, was probably strengthened through his first years in Flanders, where a great variety of intellectual and cultural influences crossed paths. Nonetheless, Góis never condemned the flourishing Portuguese industry of slave trafficking and casually reflects the anti-Semitism of the age.

Wishing to further his scholarly background, Góis enrolled in the University of Louvain (Flanders) in 1532. There he had opportunity to meet the Spaniard Juan Luis Vives, another dedicated Iberian humanist.[9] As mentor Góis chose Cornelius Grapheus, friend of Erasmus of Rotterdam and a former prisoner of the newly-established Flemish Inquisition. Grapheus instructed Góis in Latin, as well as art and music. Another influence on Góis at the time was John Magnus, the exiled Catholic archbishop of Sweden. He not only encouraged Góis' first publication, the Latin *Legatio Magni Indorum Imperatoris*, but also helped ease Góis' somewhat justified anxiety over his imperfect Latin.[10] In 1533 he visited Erasmus in Freiburg, then declined an invitation from King João to return to Portugal as a teacher of humanistic studies. The following year Góis returned to Freiburg, spending five months as the guest of Erasmus.

At this time André de Resende, a Portuguese poet and humanist also in residence at Louvain, returned to

Portugal.[11] There he availed himself of King João's open embrace of humanism to teach at the new Colégio das Artes in the university city of Coimbra. João had even invited Erasmus to Coimbra, though the visit was never realized. Until his death, João remained a supporter of humanists like Damião de Góis and of learning in general. Since the mid-fifteenth century Portuguese monarchs had encouraged classical studies of Greek and Latin texts – mostly history, poetry, and rhetoric – by inviting foreign intellectuals to Lisbon and offering scholarships to Paris, Florence, and other Italian cities. The Fleming Cleynaert, for example, was brought to the court in 1533 as master-tutor of the infante Dom Henrique. Humanist teaching and writing in Portugal was largely Erasmian, although other veins flourished as well. João also sponsored (directly and indirectly) the work of physicians, engineers, astronomers, and cartographers.[12] The introduction of Renaissance painting was also achieved through travel grants and the reception of foreign talent. During the fifteenth and sixteenth centuries the foremost Portuguese painters included Nuno Gonçalves, Grão Vasco, Fernando Henriques, Gregório Lopes, and Cristóvão de Figueiredo. Around 1500, especially, an influx of Flemish painters strengthened the art in Portugal.[13] Francisco da Holanda (1517/18-1584) studied art in Florence thanks to the patronage of João III. His contacts with the likes of Michelangelo are reflected in his treatise on aesthetics, *Da pintura antiga*.

Even as João furthered the humanist tradition, he was pressured by the Vatican's Counter Reformation, and it was during João's reign that the institution of the Inquisition was firmly planted in Portugal. Upon João's death in 1557, the inquisitor general, his brother Cardinal Henrique, became regent to his young nephew Sebastião, and only a few years later, in 1564, Portugal became the only western European nation to adopt without restrictions the rigid new edicts of the Council of Trent.[14]

INTRODUCTION

Upon the advice of Erasmus, Góis settled in Padua for further studies in 1534. In Italy he would establish a long-term friendship with the reform cardinal Bembo. During his four years in Padua Góis also made the brief acquaintance of Simão Rodrigues, a zealous Portuguese cleric who had journeyed to Italy to receive orders with the very first group of Ignatius Loyola's Jesuits. Rodrigues rose to prominence in Portugal during the 1540s, denouncing Góis as a freethinking heretic first in 1545 and again in 1550. These acts had little immediate impact, but certainly set the stage for the reopening of the case against Góis in 1571, which would lead to his conviction. Unfortunate as this chance acquaintance in Padua proved to be for Góis, Rodrigues himself was eventually deemed too volatile by his own Society of Jesus, which expelled him from Portugal in 1554.[15]

In 1538 Góis returned from Italy to Louvain, where he married Joana de Hargen. She, like Góis' maternal ancestors in Portugal, was Dutch. Góis continued his studies, but was taken prisoner by the invading French in 1542, just as he attempted to mediate the crisis. After paying his own ransom, he was handsomely rewarded for his negotiation efforts by the Emperor Charles V.

FINAL YEARS IN LISBON

Three years later King João called Góis back to Portugal. Góis settled near the Castle of São Jorge in Lisbon with his wife and three young sons, enjoying an appointment as royal historian at the Torre do Tombo, the national archives.

The role of historian would be Góis' longest and his last. During the next twenty years he produced three important works: the *Urbis Olisiponis Descriptio* (1554), translated here; the *Chronicle of the Most Fortunate King Manuel* (1566-67); and the *Chronicle of Prince João II* (1567). The latter two were written in Portuguese.

Although Góis' histories reflected a clear allegiance to the Portuguese state, his personal behavior came under greater criticism. Góis became involved in disputes with some of his contemporaries, who harshly judged him as a dangerous, irreverent outsider to Portuguese society. His many years overseas, his foreign-born wife, his cosmopolitan ways and passion for music and feasts – these bred increasing jealousy and suspicion.

More than anything, Góis' strong links with Protestant reformers during his earlier years abroad led to his final, humiliating downfall. In 1571 the Inquisition once again reviewed the case against Góis, this time calling him before the inquisitorial board. During his lengthy trial a number of witnesses testified to his apparent sympathy for Protestants and also to alleged acts of sacrilege.[16] Góis had few substantial defenses. His final plea reflects his physical and emotional degradation in the face of the Inquisition's organized opposition:

> I am in such poor shape, and not from just one sickness but rather three, which are – spells of confusion, bad kidneys, and scabies, a kind of leprosy – that anyone who comes to see me close up will be moved to pity, because there is nothing healthy at all in my body.[17]

By December of 1572 Góis had been convicted as a heretic and was imprisoned in the monastery of Batalha, north of the capital. Old and ill, he was set free sometime later and died under strange circumstances in 1574. The official version of his death depicts him as having fallen into a fireplace late at night, at an inn. However, when his remains were transferred in 1941, an analysis revealed a cranial fracture, confirming for some the hypothesis that Damião de Góis was murdered.

GÓIS' WORKS

The great majority of Góis' works were written in Latin. These texts were invariably published relatively early in the author's life – during the 1530s and 1540s – and most often in Louvain. Among them are treatises on Ethiopia and its religion, a description of Lapland, another of Hispania (including both Spain and Portugal), and an edition of letters to and from friends overseas. In addition to his published histories, letters, and essays, Góis also left several manuscripts, among them a study of musical theory, some motets, and a madrigal. Góis was generally respected by intellectuals of his time, despite his imperfect Latin.[18]

Of Góis' Portuguese-language texts the most important are the two *crónicas* of the lives of Kings Manuel and João II (1566-67, 1567, Lisbon). Góis had also written a treatise on Cicero (thereby identifying himself as a humanist) published in 1538 as *Livro de Marco Tullio Ciceram, chamado Catam maior*, in Venice.

Góis' description of Lisbon was written only four years before the death of João III. Its upbeat appraisal of the city, in a tone of frank patriotism, reflects the harmony Góis felt with the royal establishment. When Cardinal Henrique assumed the throne later that decade this relationship became more ambiguous. Henrique had in 1544 (as inquisitor general) blocked the entry into Portugal of a pamphlet published abroad by Góis, in which the author defended the Ethiopian Moors. (The Index of Prohibited Books would appear in 1547.) As regent, Henrique approved the censorship of Góis' chronicle of Manuel, forcing a second, less critical edition to be published.[19] As historian Góis produced enthusiastic prose, but tended to ramble, losing focus and reverting to formulaic descriptions of military events. If his weakness was stylistic, his strength was surely the objectivity that inspired his writing.[20]

Editions of Góis' collected Portuguese correspondence were first published in the late nineteenth century by several Portuguese academics interested in reviving scholarship on him. Góis' work had remained largely unstudied (with the exception of occasional reprints and translations)

since his death. Those scholars include Joaquim de
Vasconcellos, Guilherme Henriques, and J.M. Sousa Viterbo.

THE URBIS OLISIPONIS
DESCRIPTIO

THE BOOK

Damião de Góis' description of Lisbon was originally pub-
lished in 1554 as *Urbis Olisiponis Descriptio* by André de
Burgos, a prominent printer in the city of Évora, east of
Lisbon. Of this first edition, seventeen copies are known
to exist, including one each at the libraries of Cambridge
University and the James Ford Bell Library at the Univer-
sity of Minnesota. The other extant copies are found in
Lisbon's Biblioteca Nacional, the library of Lisbon's Palácio
Galveias, the library of Ajuda (Portugal), the library of Dom
Manuel II, Vila Viçosa (Portugal), the Biblioteca Nacional
of Madrid, the library of the Monastery of Escorial (Spain),
the Bibliothèque Nationale of Paris, the Biblioteca
Vallicelliana in Rome, the university libraries of Basel,
Erlangen, Freiburg-im-Brisgau, Heidelberg, and Leiden, a
private library in Brazil, and possibly the Prussian State
Library of Berlin. Subsequent editions appeared in 1602
(at Cologne), 1603 (Frankfurt) and 1791 (Coimbra), and it
is estimated that the work therefore appears in approximately seventy collections around the world.[21]

In 1937 the original Latin text was again published, this
time with a Portuguese translation by Raúl Machado. In
1989, José da Felicidade Alves made a second translation
into Portuguese, published by Livros Horizonte as
Descrição da Cidade de Lisboa. In his introduction he praises
Machado's translation as "very beautiful" for "avoiding a
strictly literal or servile" interpretation.[22] The translation
rendered by Felicidade Alves adheres more closely to the
original. In the selection of which Portuguese text to

translate into English, this difference became an important criterion. Since every translation may be expected to engender imprecision, however slight, in translating from a translation it is desirable that the first be as faithful to the original as possible. Because it is Felicidade Alves' version that more closely follows Góis' Latin, it has been selected here as the base text.[23]

Urbis Olisiponis Descriptio was originally published without any breaks or divisions throughout its twenty-four, unnumbered leaves, bound in three signatures, a^8, b^8, and c^8. Each full page contains twenty-eight lines of text, measuring 151 x 85 mm on the page. The title page (ai) reads:

VRBIS OLISIPONIS DE/SCRIPTIO PER DAMIA/NVM GOEM EQVI/TEM LVSITANVM,/ In qua obiter tractantur non nul/la de Indica nauigatione, per/ Graecos, et Poenos et Lusita/nos, diuersis tempori/bus inculcata. / 1554.[24]

On the following page (aii) appears Góis' dedication to Cardinal Henrique:

Inclyto Principi Domi/no Henrico, portugalliae infanti sacrossan/ctae ecclesiae Romanae, tituli sanctorum quatuor coronatorum cardinali meritissi/mo, Damianus Goes Eques Lusitanus. [25]

On the third page (aiii) appears the title:

VRBIS OLISIPONIS SITVS. / & figura. Damiano Goe equite Lusitano / authore. [26]

The main text follows immediately, without breaks. The colophon reads:

EBORAE. APVD ANDREAM / Burgesem, typographum illustrissimi prin/cipis Henrici Infantis Portugalliae, S.R.E. / Cardinalis, ac apostolice sedis Legati a latere. / Permissa est editio a reuerendo patre fra/tre Gaspare de Regisb' S. Theologie do/ctore ac heretice prauitatis inquisitore. / Mense octobri. 1554. [27]

In his Portuguese version of the text, Felicidade Alves inserted several subheadings, many of which have been retained here in the English translation. The resulting, four-part structure makes visible Góis' design and covers the following topics.

THE CONTENTS

I. HISTORY AND ENVIRONS. Lisbon and Seville, Queens of the Oceans; the Discovery of the Maritime Route to India; Maritime Knowledge of the Ancients; the Portuguese Voyages; the Founding and Naming of Lisbon; Sintra and Colares; Tritons and Sirens; Ancient History of Lisbon; the Christian Reconquest; Afonso Henriques, the Portuguese Nation, and the Flag; the Taking of Lisbon from the Moors; the Relics of Saint Vincent and the Sé Cathedral; the Chapel of Saint Anthony; the Tagus Estuary; the Other Side of the Tagus; Up the Right Bank of the Tagus.

II. AROUND THE CITY WALLS, FROM BELÉM TO THE GATE OF THE CROSS. Belém; Santos-o-Velho to São Roque; from São Roque to Our Lady of the Mount; from Graça down to the Riverbank; Overall Appearance; the City Center; Fountains and Springs.

III. SEVEN MAGNIFICENT BUILDINGS. First, the Church of the Misericórdia; Second, the All Saints Hospital; Third, the Estaus Palace; Fourth, the Public Granary; Fifth, the New Custom House; Sixth, the Ceuta House and the India House; Seventh, the War Armory.

IV. FINAL SALUTE. Up the Tagus to Santarém; Alenquer, "My Birthplace!"; the Tagus Reigns over the World; Conclusion.

Although the *Urbis Olisiponis Descriptio* reflects certain historical truths about sixteenth-century Lisbon – the city's layout, a quick accounting of municipal divisions and religious orders – it was not Damião de Góis the historian who wrote it, but rather Góis the good-humored, well-traveled humanist. Designed to be an entertaining tour guide of Lisbon for Góis' friends visiting from elsewhere in Europe, it indulges in the humanists' appreciation of classical traditions, even when at the expense of truth. For example, the part of the first section that accompanies the seaborne reader entering the Tagus estuary calls attention to both ancient and modern sightings of "marine-men," or tritons. Góis was simply too experienced and educated for us to take at face value his endorsement of these anecdotes. Elsewhere he presents other handsome exaggerations, or outright lies, with or without classical references. When he claims to have seen "the majority" of all foreign arsenals located in Europe and Asia (and in this way knows them to be inferior to those of the Portuguese), he asks us to forget that he never left Europe. When Góis describes Lisbon's water supply in nearly ecstatic terms, he is lying preposterously. Other accounts show that the few public fountains were filthy, chaotic, and usually dangerous.[28]

Although we cannot always accept as truth the words of the *Urbis Olisiponis Descriptio*, we certainly gain an impressionistic appreciation for the reality they depict. Clearly, Góis gives us a strong sense for the layout and topography of Lisbon and describes the people of the city in vibrant terms. Viewed from Almada, across the Tagus, "the shape of the city resembles that of a fish bladder" (under the subheading "Overall Appearance"). Several valleys of the city "take on the shape of the letter 'delta' as they flow out toward the sea, rolling across different lands and resembling an oxskin, without the tail" (under "Second Building"). Through his enthusiastic eyes we see the Rua Nova de Mercadores (New Merchants Street) in downtown Lisbon. It is "...much wider than the others and adorned on both sides with exquisite buildings. Every day merchants representing almost every people and region of the world flock together here, joined by great throngs of people enjoying the advantages of business at the port" (under "Third Building").

While Góis goes to great lengths to polish the image of Lisbon and Portugal, thereby entertaining and impressing his reader, he also provides criticism. When he points out that Lisbon's professional letter-writers are unique in all of Europe, he is slyly calling Lisbon a city of illiterates.[29] It must be remembered that Góis only reluctantly returned to his homeland from a far more comfortable and cultured milieu abroad, in Flanders. His inflated pride in Portugal's empire is tempered with this disappointment, perhaps even bitterness, in the reality of Lisbon.

Góis also makes two specific criticisms of a civic nature. In describing the Third Building, the Estaus Palace, he notes that it was built with the "nation's treasuries" by Prince Pedro, whose "only intention was to offer lodging to ambassadors of foreign nations and their kings, who were received there at public expense, with all high pomp and honors." Later, writing about the Ribeira Market near the Alfândega Nova (New Custom House), he condemns the government's high rental fees for fish baskets, calling it "veiled tyranny." Only a few years later Damião de Góis would release a bit-more-substantial political criticism in his history of King Manuel. Never, however, did Góis publicly dissent on truly major issues.

The *Urbis Olisiponis Descriptio*, then, may be seen as a mixture of hard fact and exaggerations of convenience. As such it is a natural distillation of at least two literary currents born in the Middle Ages and inherited by Góis in the sixteenth century: the fairly straightforward urban register and the more florid *laus civitatis*, or "city praise." A discussion of each follows.

THE URBIS OLISIPONIS DESCRIPTIO AS URBAN REGISTER

Since the Middle Ages, Europeans had been rediscovering the Greek and Roman tradition of describing and analyzing the world, both local and faraway. As Latinized editions of classical texts returned to medieval Europe,[30] imposing a stronger geographical sensibility among readers, travel itself was becoming much more common. Through the Crusades and through the rise of enterprising trading cities such as Genoa, Pisa, and Venice, people gained greater perspective and insight regarding their own locale. Not surprisingly, written accounts of countryside, towns, and cities began to grow in the twelfth century. These descriptions of locales and regions – known generically as chorography – included at least three basic kinds: the itinerary (typically for pilgrims), the field terrier (a minutely detailed accounting of local land divisions), and the urban register or survey (a factual listing of a city's religious, professional, or demographic subdivisions).

The last of these, the urban register, grew during the Renaissance to become an especially important tool for politicians and royalty. Typically a high-ranking local authority would commission the document as a report on overall population (a census), numbers of individuals in all occupations, resident foreigners, and ecclesiastical wealth by church, monastery, and convent. Such a document was written in 1527 for Rome,[31] (providing a snapshot of the city just before its sack), while in Lisbon two appeared just prior to the publication of Góis' 1554 description of the city.[32] Even after the invention of printing, these projects rarely appeared as books. Instead, they were manuscripts meant for few readers.

The careful documentation found in much of Góis' *Urbis Olisiponis Descriptio* reflects this medieval and Renaissance tradition of the urban register. The environs of Lisbon (Sintra, Colares, Cabo da Roca, etc.) are enumerated, often with distances. Terrain and minerals are described. The city's seven featured buildings are reported to house various religious orders, or to donate (in the case of the Misericórdia) "the sum of forty-thousand ducats" to the poor, or to contain a very particular stock of weapons or precious commodities. These descriptions are often minutely presented.

THE URBIS OLISIPONIS DESCRIPTIO AS LAUS CIVITATIS

Although the *Urbis Olisiponis Descriptio* certainly reflects its heritage as a kind of urban register, its style is crafted after another, quite different tradition, of the *laudes civitatum,* or simply *laudes.*[33] The roots of this genre are, strictly speaking, ancient, dating to a eulogy of Athens by the second-century Greek rhetorician Aelius Aristides. Few Roman city-praises were written. By late antiquity, a treatise on the genre itself was composed and partially preserved in a slightly later, eighth-century manuscript, *De laudibus urbium.* Its anonymous author dictates the terms of the *laus,* which must describe "the dignity of the [city's] founder... the aspect of the walls, the region and the site," important natural resources, ornaments, and any nobility of note. Mention should be made of nearby, noteworthy cities, presumably to heighten the prestige of the city being described in the *laus.*[34]

The first medieval *laus* also appears, perhaps not surprisingly, during the eighth century. The *Versum de Mediolano civitate* (c. 740) follows the prescriptions of *De laudibus urbium* in praising the city of Milan. Another *laus* appears shortly thereafter, describing Verona. The *laus* was primarily an Italian tradition that grew especially strong as the independent *comuni* of northern Italy came into their own during the twelfth and thirteenth centuries. Naturally enough, the *laus* reflected a heightened civic pride. *Laudes* were also composed in either prose or verse for other important cities in Europe and the Mediterranean region. Among these are Master Gregory's *De Mirabilibus Urbis Romae* (1150-1200, Rome), William Fitzstephen's *Descriptio Nobilissimae Civitatis Londoniae* (1173-74, London), Bonvesin della Riva's *De Magnalibus Urbis Mediolani* (1288, Milan), and the *Recommendatio Civitatis Parisiensis* (1323, Paris). The medieval authors of these works faced a fundamental problem of organization: while a chronicle or biography could be narrated linearly, through time, a city could be described in many different ways.[35] Little exposed to classical Greek and Latin models, their *laudes* were somewhat poorly organized and rather mechanical in tone – occasionally more akin, perhaps, to the typical (if shorter) urban register. The Latin of these early *laudes* was a vehicle of information, but not necessarily of style.

During the fourteenth century the character of the *laudes* began to change. Among the Italian cities political and commercial shifts eroded the more insular sensibility that had earlier given rise to their *laudes*. Simultaneously, the seeds of humanism were being sown in literature. Therefore, from the beginning of the fifteenth century the *laus* was increasingly an exercise in the humanist concern with ancient Greek and Roman models. While earlier *laudes* showed a more authentic local pride (though by no means a naive patriotism), the Renaissance *laudes* were opportunities for their authors to exhibit erudition and a mastery of classical rhetoric while praising their cities.[36]

One of the most polished of this new kind of *laudes* was written in 1403 by the Florentine humanist Leonardo Bruni. His *Laudatio Florentinae Urbis* was consciously modeled after the Greek Aristides, specifically for the city's external circumstances, physical attributes, and qualities of character. Bruni's *Laudatio* is exceptional not only for his incorporation of Latin stylistics and clearer organization, but also for his foray into the political thought which, in a sense, his Renaissance Florence embodied. A sample:

> There are in this city the most talented men, who easily surpass the limits of other men in whatever they do. Whether they follow the military profession, or devote

themselves to the task of governing the commonwealth, or to certain studies or to the pursuit of knowledge, or to commerce – in everything they undertake and in every activity they far surpass all other mortals, nor do they yield first place in any field to any other nation. They are patient in their labor, ready to meet danger, ambitious for glory, strong in counsel, industrious, generous, elegant, pleasant, affable, and above all, urbane.[37]

Others in this newer line of *laudes* included Giannozzo Manetti's *Laudatio Ianuensium* (1444, Genoa), Leon Battista Alberti's *Descriptio Romae* (1440s, Rome), and Pierre Gilles' *Urbis Constantinopolitanae Descriptio* (1552, Constantinople). Damião de Góis' *Urbis Olisiponis Descriptio* was heir to this line of fifteenth- and sixteenth-century *laudes*. As a humanist, Góis took up his *laudes* because that genre had come to be, by 1554, part of the humanist literary realm.

One of the central humanist goals was to cultivate and interpret connections to the ancients. Most *laudes* – after Bruni's in 1403 – did indeed make frequent references to classical topics. Góis' *Urbis Olisiponis Descriptio* is no exception. The author takes great pains to describe Lisbon not only as a former Roman colony, but also as a favorite of Greek and Roman writers, whose judgment, we are to assume, was impeccable. In treating the question of whether Ulysses founded and gave his name to Lisbon, Góis presents evidence on both sides in a rational, even legalistic way.[38] Inevitably, he agrees with Strabo's endorsement of the Ulysses theory, saying, "I am more satisfied, however, to agree with the opinion of an illustrious writer such as he than adopt the ideas of naysayers who scoff at him without any solid argument of their own."[39] To convey the esteem in which ancient writers held the natural resources of Lusitania, Góis quotes Justin:

> Many authors recounted that in Lusitania, along the Tagus River, the mares conceive through the wind alone. Such legends derive from the mares' great fertility and from

the quantity of herds; these are so numerous in Galicia
and in Lusitania, and they run so speedily, that they seem
in fact to have been conceived by the wind itself.[40]

Justin actually concludes that Lisbon is not magical, but
"merely" abounds in extraordinary wildlife. Although Góis
eventually refuses to pass verdict on the issue, he has
clearly succeeded in polishing the image of the region of
Lisbon.

It is not only the content of the *Urbis Olisiponis Descriptio* that distinguishes it as a humanist text of persuasion.
In addition, many sections are rendered in a declamatory
tone – in Latin, of course – implicitly paying homage to
the classical tradition of rhetoric. Reviewing the history of
Portuguese discoveries, Góis writes, "Let us take as our
point of departure the one who, with the greatest will
power and strength of spirit, threw himself into an undertaking so noble for our times. He was the unvanquished
son of Dom Afonso V, the glorious King of Portugal, Dom
João II."[41] Later, writing about the founding of Portugal
by its first king, Afonso Henriques, Góis' prose becomes
charged and dramatic: "Our own writers recount that,
before entering battle, this same Afonso saw Christ in the
skies, nailed to the cross and promising him victory. The
king, inflamed with faith, responded with these words:
'Lord, it is not necessary that you appear before me, for I
firmly believe that you are the Son of God....'"[42]

Turning to other works, Lisbon was also the subject of
at least two humanist poems, both written to honor the
city. Girolamo Britonio wrote the "Ulysbonae regiae
Lusitaniae carmen" (1546); and in 1636, only four years
before Lisbon would regain its role as imperial capital from
the Spanish, Gabriel Pereira de Castro wrote the epic
"Ulyssea ou Lysboa edificada." André de Resende's
"Vincentius levita et martyr"[43] also treated the Ulysses
theme in Lisbon's history.

MAPS AND VIEWS OF LISBON

The *Urbis Olisiponis Descriptio* takes on greater value when one remembers that the catastrophic earthquake of 1755 destroyed much of the city center that we come to know through this text. Góis' documentation of the steep streets and contemporary buildings may be understood more completely by referring to views and maps of the city. Pictorial descriptions of Lisbon during the sixteenth century certainly enrich Damião de Góis' colorful presentation, but few remain. During the first half of the century, António Godinho vividly illuminated two manuscript pages with scenes of Lisbon as viewed from the Tagus. They show the bustling *terreiro do paço,* or Palace Square (now Praça do Comércio), as well as city gates and other features also visited by Góis in the *Urbis Olisiponis Descriptio.* A third, similar view can be seen in the *Crónica de D. Afonso Henriques,* painted by Duarte Galvão. Yet another appears in the *Genealogia do Infante Dom Fernando de Portugal.*

These views are all oblique, or bird's-eye, perspectives, as was the custom since the Middle Ages. Other informative and attractive oblique views of the sixteenth century include the 1541 woodcut inserted into the Sebastian Münster *Cosmographia* and the masterly, number-coded view published at Cologne in 1598 in Braun and Hogenberg's *Civitates orbis terrarum.* By 1650 the João Nunes Tinoco overhead scale map provided even more accurate information for the layout of the pre-quake city.

The calamity of the earthquake was followed by an ambitious, Neoclassical redesign of the Baixa and other devastated zones, and two excellent maps survive from that third quarter of the eighteenth century. One uses a yellow and red overlay scheme to effectively compare pre- and post-quake Lisbon. In the other, from 1778, Tomás López drew a magnificent 3' x 5' map of all of Portugal ("Mapa General del Reyno de Portugal," Madrid) that includes the gracious touch of an extensive bibliography of his sources. The 1598 Braun and Hogenberg map has been chosen here to accompany Damião de Góis' tour of Lisbon. It was probably engraved on a copperplate during the 1570s or 1580s, possibly by Frans Hogenberg. The 140 numbered and labeled buildings allow the modern traveler or researcher the privilege of identifying very nearly the exact location of the most important buildings of sixteenth-century, Renaissance Lisbon.[44] There is evidence, furthermore, that the map and the *Urbis Olisiponis Descriptio* were linked even four hundred years ago: the other side of the map carries Latin text clearly inspired by Góis' 1554 publication.

The Braun and Hogenberg view is neither map nor picture, strictly speaking, but carries qualities of both. With its inviting, bird's-eye perspective and a form of representation that slides unexpectedly between two and three dimensions, it is part truth, part fantasy. As such it may be the most appropriate complement to a reading of Damião de Góis' *Urbis Olisiponis Descriptio*.[45]

NOTES

1. Much of this introduction's biographical information comes from an excellent study of Góis and his era: Elizabeth Feist Hirsch, *Damião de Góis: The Life and Thought of a Portuguese Humanist* (The Hague: Martinus Nijhoff, 1967). Readers with a special interest in the life of Góis, as well as his humanist connections in Europe, should consult this work. Its bibliography is especially useful, as it includes the many major and minor published references to him up to 1967. For a minutely cross-referenced guide to Góis' Latin letters – with facing Portuguese translations – see Amadeu Torres, *As Cartas Latinas de Damião de Góis* (Paris: Fundação Calouste Gulbenkian, Centro Cultural Português, 1982). Many of those letters were addressed to the preeminent humanist and contemporary of Góis – Erasmus of Rotterdam – and reflect Góis' religious concerns and influences.

2. Although Góis never mentions Gil Vicente (1465-1536), it is very likely that he witnessed Vicente's famous *autos* as a child, and that those celebrated works of this period's most famous dramatist helped instill in him a reform outlook. Vicente wrote forty plays, many of them in Castilian, a practice common among Portuguese writers since the fourteenth century. The four major dramatic modes in Vicente's work were described by Aubrey Bell as religious, patriotic-imperial, satirical and pastoral. For a translation and study, see Gil Vicente, *Four Plays of Gil Vicente*, ed. and trans. Aubrey Bell (Cambridge: Cambridge University Press, 1920; rprnt., New York: Kraus Reprint, 1969).

3. Vasco da Gama rounded the Cape of Good Hope and sailed on to Goa, India, in 1498. By 1522 Portuguese vessels freely sailed as far east as present-day Indonesia. Major outposts at this time included El Mina (or Guiné), Sofala, Hormuz, Cochin and Goa, Melaka, and the Moluccas. The Portuguese pattern of empire-building excluded outright colonization, unlike the Spaniards.

The network of heavily defended *feitorias* served to extract and export the wealth gleaned from conquered coastal lands overseas. See Lyle N. McAlister, *Spain and Portugal in the New World, 1492-1700* (Minneapolis: University of Minnesota Press, 1984), 251-57; and James C. Boyajian, *Portuguese Trade in Asia under the Hapsburgs, 1580-1640* (Baltimore: Johns Hopkins University Press, 1993), 1-17.

4.   Arab merchants had plied the Indian Ocean, delivering goods to Venetian traders at Red Sea and Persian Gulf ports. From there these luxury items were shipped to the principal European port cities for distribution inland. The Portuguese designs on the Venetian business into Europe were furthered in 1453 by the Ottoman Turk occupation of Constantinople, until then a key point for Venetian shippers.

5.   For much of the fifteenth century the heavily fortified *feitoria* of São Jorge da Mina – El Mina – in the Gulf of Guinea provided the bulk of wealth, in both gold and slaves. African slaves were first taken to Lisbon in 1441 and were forced to provide much of the labor required in the radical transformation of Lisbon's port district into the center of a maritime empire. Slaves from India were also taken, though less so. Foreign visitors to Lisbon during the fifteenth and sixteenth centuries commonly commented on the many races seen throughout the city. For details on the circumstances of one celebrated African in Lisbon, see A.C. de C.M. Saunders, "The Life and Humour of João de Sá Panasco, o Negro, Former Slave, Court Jester and Gentleman of the Portugal Royal Household (fl. 1524-1567)," in F.W. Hodcroft, D.G. Pattison, et al., *Medieval and Renaissance Studies on Spain and Portugal in Honour of P.E. Russell* (Oxford: Society for the Study of Medieval Languages and Literatures, 1981), 180-91.

6.   The expedition's leader, Pedro Álvares Cabral, named it *Ilha da Vera Cruz*, or Island of the True Cross, having no knowledge of the extent of South America. Some historians have speculated that Portugal knew of the landmass through African contacts as early as 1494, when at Tordesillas, Spain, it negotiated to extend the proposed line of demarcation further west, resulting in their future claim to Brazil.

7. For example, Góis once advised João III to be wary when dealing with Venetian traders, whose guile he apparently witnessed firsthand. Their aim, he warned, was to cut Portuguese trade receipts. Later Góis would defend João to Italian critics. Although privately critical of royal fiscal policy in the spice markets, Góis was perhaps the premiere apologist throughout Europe of Portugal's monopolistic practices.

8. England, along with France, had at this time made only tentative voyages in search of new markets abroad. By Góis' death in 1574, these two nations had begun their rise toward imperial power just when Portugal, and less so Spain, had begun to suffer the consequences of overspending during their extraordinarily ambitious first phase of expansion. If England's defeat of the Spanish Armada in 1588 symbolized the coming decline for Spain, Portugal's far more dramatic losses were signaled in the catastrophic Moroccan crusade of 1578 at Alcácer Quibir. Approximately 20,000 Christians were killed or imprisoned, among them their erratic young king, Sebastião (1554-1578). With the throne unoccupied, in 1580 Portugal was subsumed by Spain, then led by Philip II. Only sixty years later, in the restoration of 1640, would the Portuguese regain their independence.

9. For more on Juan Luis Vives, see Robert P. Adams, *The Better Part of Valor: More, Erasmus, Colet and Vives on Humanism, War and Peace 1496-1535* (Seattle: University of Washington Press, 1962); Carlos Noreña, *Juan Luis Vives* (The Hague: Martinus Nijhoff, 1970); Marian Leona Tobriner, SNJN, Vives' Introduction to Wisdom: *A Renaissance Textbook* (New York: Columbia University-Teacher's College Press, 1968); and William H. Woodward, *Studies in Education during the Age of the Renaissance, 1400-1600* (New York: Columbia University Press, 1967), 180-210.

10. According to António José Saraiva and Oscar Lopes, *História da literatura portuguesa* (Lisbon: Publicações Europa-América, 1980), 294, Góis' Latin was "not always his and not always impeccable." For specific criticisms see the 1937 translation of Góis' *Urbis Olisiponis Descriptio* in Raúl Machado, *Lisboa de Quinhentos* (Lisbon: Livraria Avelar Machado, 1937). Regarding Góis' style in his Portuguese-language histories, see note 20.

11. For Resende's Portuguese works, see *Obras portuguesas de André de Resende*, ed. José Pereira Tavares (Lisbon: Sá da Costa, n.d.) For some of his Latin poetry and correspondence, with English translation, see *On Court Life*, ed. and trans. John R.C. Martyn (Bern: Peter Lang, 1990).

12. For a treatment of Spanish and Portuguese intellectual and creative activity during the Renaissance, see Miguel Batllori, *Humanismo y Renacimiento: Estudios hispano-europeos* (Barcelona: Ariel, 1987).

13. An excellent, bilingual reference is José Luis Porfírio, *Pintura Portuguesa-Portuguese Painting: Museu Nacional de Arte Antiga* (Lisbon: Quetzal, 1991). Also see Dagoberto Markl and Fernando António Baptista Pereira, *História da Arte em Portugal* (Lisbon: Alfa, 1986). A complementary work is Jonathan Brown and Richard G. Mann, *Spanish Painting of the Fifteenth through Nineteenth Centuries* (Washington, DC: National Gallery of Art, 1990).

14. Saraiva and Lopes, 183.

15. For more on this early phase of Jesuit history, and Portugal's place within it, see John W. O'Malley, SJ, *The First Jesuits* (Cambridge, MA and London: Harvard University Press, 1993), 30-32, 188, 329-34.

16. An acquaintance testified that Góis and his household served pork at a Saturday dinner. According to this witness, Góis had made the off-color, blasphemous joke that the dinner's offense wasn't so much the pork that entered his mouth as the vile form it later took. From Raul Rêgo, ed., *O processo de Damião de Góis na Inquisição* (Lisbon: Edições Excelsior, 1971), 160-61. For an account of the trial of an Englishman in the early seventeenth century, see Mary Brearley, *Hugo Gurgeny: Prisoner of the Lisbon Inquisition* (New Haven: Yale University Press, 1948). Two complementary texts are William Monter, *Frontiers of Heresy: The Spanish Inquisition from the Basque Lands to Sicily* (Cambridge & New York: Cambridge University Press, 1990); and Ángel Alcalá, *El proceso inquisitorial de Fray Luis de León* (Salamanca: Junta de Castilla y León, 1991).

17. "Eu estou tão mal disposto, e não de uma só doença senão de três, que são – vertigo, rins e sarna, como especie de lepra –

que qualquer pessoa que me vir se for próximo se moverá à piedade porque em meu corpo não há coisa sã." Excerpted from "Carta do reu" ("Letter from the Defendant"), in Rêgo, 208-9.

18. For additional information on both Latin and Portuguese works by Góis, see Appendix A, and also the annotated bibliography in Hirsch, 225-32.

19. Góis had told unflattering truths about members of the nobility. He also criticized Manuel's rejection of Fernão de Magalhães – Ferdinand Magellan – which had led to the latter's circumnavigation of the globe under the Spanish flag. (Magellan himself was killed in the Philippines during that voyage, but his crew sailed on.) Overall, the chronicle of Manuel was consistently positive.

20. Góis' *crónicas* are considered faithful, if bland, histories. Saraiva and Lopes, 294-95, call Góis "a conscientious historian" whose tremendous objectivity resulted in a "colorless style" that couldn't "give life to characters, discover the passions and weaknesses of the protagonists…nor express collective national movements." More celebrated Portuguese historians prior to Góis included Fernão Lopes, Gomes Eanes de Zurara, and Rui de Pina. João de Barros and Fernão Lopes de Castanheda were highly respected contemporaries of Góis.

21. All information relating to the various editions of the *Urbis Olisiponis Descriptio* owes to José da Felicidade Alves, *Descrição da Cidade de Lisboa* (Lisbon: Livros Horizonte, 1988), 16-19.

22. Felicidade Alves, 19.

23. Felicidade Alves used a copy of the original, 1554, edition in making his 1989 translation to the Portuguese. He notes that a second translation was necessitated only because of difficulties in obtaining rights to re-publish Machado's first.

24. A Description of the City of Lisbon by Damião de Góis, Portuguese gentleman, in which he deals in passing with several voyages at various times to India by the Greeks, the Phoenicians and the Portuguese.

25. To the famous prince Dom Henrique, Infante of Portugal,

most worthy titular cardinal of the church of SS. Quattro Coronati, of the Most Holy Roman Church. Damião de Góis, Portuguese gentleman.

26. The site and appearance of the city of Lisbon, written by Damião de Góis, Portuguese gentleman.

27. Évora, at the press of Andre de Burgos, printer of the most illustrious Prince Henrique, the Infante of Portugal, Cardinal of the Holy Roman Church, and Legate of the Apostolic See. This edition authorized by the Reverend Father Gaspar dos Reis, Doctor of Sacred Theology and Inquisitor of Heretical Depravity. October 1554.

28. Fernando Castelo-Branco, *Lisboa Seiscentista* (Lisbon: Câmara Municipal, 1956), 375-76. See also the essay by Irisalva Moita in *Lisboa Quinhentista* (exhibition catalog, Lisbon: Câmara Municipal, 1983), 14. According to her, "Lisbon was, in spite of its wealth and magnificence, a filthy city...." She refers to the complaints of the painter Francisco de Holanda, a contemporary of Góis who lived for several years in the cities of Renaissance Italy. Holanda describes not only inferior water supplies in Lisbon, but a lack of monumentality in its buildings, as well as too few paved sidewalks. See Francisco de Holanda, *Da Fábrica que falece à cidade de Lisboa*, ed. Joaquim Vasconcelos (Porto: Imprensa Portuguesa, 1875).

29. I am indebted to José da Felicidade Alves for clarifying to me Damião de Góis' point of view at this and other places throughout the text. See also below, p. 52 n. 82.

30. Many such texts were translated from Greek or Arabic in Toledo during the twelfth century. Ptolemy's extraordinarily influential *Geography* reappeared in Latin through an easterly route, in 1406.

31. *Descriptio Urbis: The Roman Census of 1527*, ed. Egmont Lee (Rome: Bulzoni Editore, 1985).

32. Cristóvão Rodrigues de Oliveira, *Lisboa em 1551: Sumário*, ed. José da Felicidade Alves (Lisbon: Livros Horizonte, 1988); and João Brandão, *Grandeza e abastança de Lisboa em 1552*, ed. José da Felicidade Alves (Lisbon: Livros Horizonte, 1990). The former

provides valuable information regarding streets and professions. The latter contains not only a great wealth of descriptive detail regarding daily life, but inflated praise for the city. For Brandão, Lisbon supersedes Venice, Cairo, Babylon, Paris, and even Rome. Overall, however, Brandão's presentation of factual material seems even-handed, and is at times even critical.

33. The genre is also referred to as *descriptio urbis* or *descriptio*.

34. This information is found in two key sources on the *laus* tradition. The first, Chiara Frugoni, *A Distant City: Images of Urban Experience in the Medieval World*, trans. William McCuaig (Princeton: Princeton University Press, 1991), provided the short translation cited here (p. 54). Its chapter "The Better City," 54-81, describes not only the roots of the *laus* genre, but an interpretation of symbols embedded in subsequent, medieval *laudes* texts. A second, excellent source is Gina Fasoli, specifically her "La coscienza civica nelle 'Laudes civitatum,'" in *La coscienza cittadina nei comuni italiani del Duecento*. Atti dell'XI Convegno del Centro di studi sulla spiritualità medievale (Todi: Accademia Tudertina, 1972), 9-44. Her article charts the changing nature of the *laus* from the early to late Middle Ages, when the genre came under humanist influence. It is quite useful toward understanding the *laus* of Lisbon written later by Damião de Góis.

35. See J.K. Hyde, "Medieval Descriptions of Cities," *Bulletin of the John Rylands Library* 48.2 (1966): 308-40.

36. Fasoli, 44.

37. From *The Humanism of Leonardo Bruni: Selected Texts*, eds. and trans. Gordon Griffiths, James Hankins, and David Thompson, Medieval and Renaissance Texts and Studies 46 (Binghamton, NY: Renaissance Society of America and SUNY Press, 1987), 121.

38. Many of the Iberian humanists of the fifteenth and sixteenth centuries were, in fact, trained in law. Ottavio Di Camillo points out in his "Humanism in Spain," in *Renaissance Humanism*, ed. Albert Rabil, Jr. (Philadelphia: University of Pennsylvania Press, 1988), 2:55-108, that Roman law had been reintroduced in Spain by approximately 1200, helping to lay a foundation for the

systematic practice of discourse, one of the hallmarks of humanism. Humanist writing in Spain and (less so) Portugal was underway by the fifteenth century, spurred by Italian models. In the same article (58) Di Camillo notes that Spanish humanism during the fifteenth century showed more respect for the vernacular – Castilian – than did any of the other variants of humanism in Europe, judging from the number of classical texts brought into Castilian translation.

39. *Urbis Olisiponis Descriptio.* See below p. 8.

40. Ibid., 9.

41. Ibid., 4.

42. Ibid., 14.

43. In *Vincentius levita et martyr,* ed. José V. de Pina Martins (Paris: Touzot, 1981).

44. This view and 59 others from the original, six-volume set of *Civitates orbis terrarum* are collected in *The City Maps of Europe. 16th Century Town Plans from Braun & Hogenberg,* ed. John Goss (Chicago: Rand McNally, 1992). All are from editions retaining their original watercolors.

45. The tricky, deceptive nature of this view was taken a step further in 1672, when an excellent copy of it was made to represent "Nowel Amsterdam en L'Amerique" – New Amsterdam. See I.N. Phelps Stokes, *The Iconography of Manhattan 1498-1909,* vol. 1 (New York: Richard H. Dodd, 1915).

OLISSIPPO quæ nunc Lisboa , civitas ...
Orientis, et multarum Insularum Apl...

Octzsu...

121. *Templum D. N. consolationis*
ante portam ferri. 122 *Templum*
Sancti Anthonij de Padua .
123 *Templum Misericordiæ .*
124 *Sacellum sancti Spiritus de alfama .*
125 *Templum Sancti Marcu . 126*
Templum sancti Blasij et sanctæ Lucæ .
127 *Templum sancti Ludouici .*
128 *Templum sancti Spiritu da pedrera .*
129 *Ermita D. N. de monte .*

... *Regias* ...
... *vulgo paco de Castella .* 2 *Pons regius* ...
vares da Ribeira . 3 *tertium regia vulgo paco dex*...
tas vbi mare est Inquisitor 4 *Sancti Eloi regij vulgo paco*...
sancti Eloi . Alia Insignia . 5 *Regium pretorium vulgo* ...
Lega . 6 *Domus frumentaria vulgo terra roe do tugo .* 7 ...
indica vetz . 8 *Domus indica nova .* 9 *Armamentarium* ...
... *Aerarium regium .* 10 *Iustitialis quæstio Sanctorij .* 11 ...
... *vulgo Regio dicitur .* 12 *Platea* ...
... *velho dicitur .* 13 *Alia nova mercatorum* ...
... *les canales derivatæ vulgo chafaris del*...
... *vulgo Ribeira .* 16 *Domus* ...
... *vulgo Limoiro dicitur .*

Castelli civitatis . 18 *Coructs , in sanitatis mortis insub*
cio nondica , vulgo alcaceua dicitur . 19 *moles Corbiti*
vulgo Caso do caruao . 20 *Fornaces ad conficiendum*
calcem . 21 *Moles lignorum vulgo Cais da madª .* 22
Lacy vbi rudentes nautici efficiuntur vulgo Cordegianus .
23 *Scholæ generales vbi antiquitus scientiæ profitebatur .*
24 *Paco de madera .* 25 *Monasterij fratrum* ...
ria fratru . 25 *Monasterium Francisci ordinis Minorum*
26 *Monast. S. Mariæ de carmo Carmelitaru .* 27 *Monast.*
Trinitatis . 28 *Monast. S. Dominici Vincentus .* 29 *Monast.*
S. Elisabeth vulgo S. Vincentius . 30 *Monast. S. Vincentes Canonici*
regularis . 31 *Mon. P. Georgi de grace , ordin. Augustin .* 32
Collegij Societ. Resu . S. Rogi . 33 *Collegij et Scholæ S. Antoni*
34 *Collegij orphanorum . Monasteria*
stantia . 35 *Monaste. Belnacortis .* 36 *Monast. D. N.*
fa . 37 *Monast. D. N. da aliciada .* 38 *Monast. D. N.*
esperanca . 39 *Monast. dos reys vbe .* 40 *Monaste.*
Sanctæ Clara . *Turres vetceres vrbe .* 41 *Por...*
ferri . 42 *Porta maris , ferres naues vbi residet da* ...
dux Comes . 43 *Porta maris ad secum .* 44 *Por...*
ta ferri vbi res ... se po certis do che ... del ...
Palicio de ferro de annes . 45 *Porta ferri* ...
46 Porta ... 47 Porta alisfi... 48 *Por... ...*
Ginesij . 48 *Porta da duos Vbiques .* 49 *Port...*
Mons . *Porte p ... nova vrbe .* 50 *Porta sanct...*
teneq; vulgo pesteygo da S. Laur ... 51 *Porta poy ...*

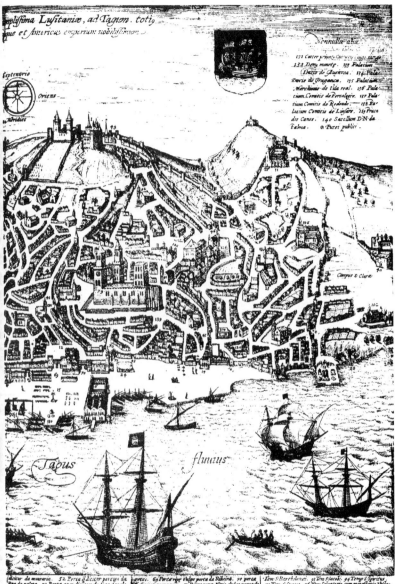

...plissima Lusitaniæ, ad Tagum. toti
...que et Americæ emporium nobilißimum.

Septentrio

Oriens

Meridies

Nonnulla alia
131 Carcer priuat. Ciuitat. 132 Palatium
132 Deni munere. 133 Palatium
(Ducis de Auenero. 134 Palat
Ducis de Braganca. 135 Palatium
Marchionis de Vila real. 136 Pala
tium Comitis de Portalegre. 137 Pala
tium Comitis de Redondo. 138 Pa
latium Comitis de Linares. 139 Puca
dis Canes. 140 Sacellum D.N. da
Palma. (.) Putei publici.

Campus S. Claræ

Tagus   fluuius

Key to Braun & Hogenberg Map

Page and map-key numbers to many of these sites are indicated in the index. Thus on page vi, the site keyed 10 is indexed as **vi: 10**. Not all sites in the key have corresponding numbers on original map.

1 Castle Palace
2 Ribeira Palace or Royal Palace
3 Estaus Palace, later of the Inquisition
4 Saint Eloy Palace
5 Customs House
6 Public Granary
7 Old India House
8 New India House
9 Old Arsenal
10 Todos Santos Hospital
11 Rossio Praça
12 Old Pillory
13 Rua Nova dos Mercadores
14 King's Fountain
15 Ribeira Praça
16 Limoeiro Prison
17 City Castle
18 Alcaçova Palace
19 Coalworks and dock
20 Limekilns
21 Lumberyard Dock, Cais de Madeira
22 The New Rope Walk
23 Escolas Geráis
24 Lumber Palace. Friars' Monastery
25 Franciscan Monastery of St. Francis
26 Monastery of St. Mary of the Carmelites
27 Monastery of the Trinity
28 Monastery of St. Dominic the Preacher
29 Monastery of St. Eloy, Order of St. John
30 Monastery of St. Vincent of Canons Regular
31 Monastery of St. Mary of Grace, Augustine Order
32 St. Rock Jesuit College
33 St. Anthony Jesuit School and College
34 Orphanage and Monastery of the Virgins
35 Monastery of the Savior
36 Monastery of Our Lady of the Rose
37 Monastery of Our Lady of the Annunciation
38 Monastery of Our Lady of Hope
39 Monastery of St. Anne
40 Monastery of St. Clare

GATES TO THE OLD CITY

41 Gate of Iron
42 Sea Gate, of the Rua das Canastias
43 Sea Gate to St. John
44 Gate of the King's Fountain
44* Postern of the Count of Linhares
45 Gate of St. Peter
46 Gate of the Sun
47 Gate of the Nursery
47* Gate of St. George
48 Gate of Dom Fadrique
49 Gate of Monis

GATES OF THE NEW CITY

50 Gate of St. Laurence
51 Gate of the Mouraria
52 Gate of the Rua da Palma
53 Gate of the Ballgame
54 Gate of St. Anne
55 Gate of St. Anthony
56 Gate of the King's Horse Stables

NOTES TO INTRODUCTION

57 Gate of St. Rock
58 Postern of the Trinity
59 Gate of St. Catharine
60 Gate of the Duke of Bragança
61 Gate of the Holy Body
62* Gate of the Cabertes
62 Gate of the Corte Reáis
63 Golden Gate
64 Gate of the Warehouse
65 Gate of the Palace Arches
66 Gate of the Mint
67 Gate of the Arch of Nails
68 Gate of the Fortress Arch
69 Gate of the Ribeira
70 Toll Gate
71 Sea Gate
72 Gate of Fountain of the
   Horses
73 Powder Gate
74 Gate of the Cross
75 Gate of St. Vincent
76 Postern of St. Vincent
77 Postern of Our Lady of Grace
78 Gate of St. Andrew
78* Postern of Alfama

PARISH CHURCHES

79 Sé Cathedral
80 Church of St. Julian
81 Church of St. Mary
   Magdalene
82 Church of Our Lady of the
   Conception
83 Church of St. Nicholas
84 Church of St. Justin
85 Church of St. Matthew
86 Church of St. Sebastian of the
   Mouraria
87 Church of St. Anthony in the
   Jesuit College
88 Church of St. Laurence
89 Church of St. Christopher
90 Church of St. Mamas
91 Church of St. George
92 Church of St. Bartholomew

93 Church of St. James
94 Church of the Holy Spirit
95 Church of the Holy Cross
96 Church of the Savior and
   Convent of Virgins
97 Church of St. Thomas
98 Church of St. Andrew
99 Church of St. Marina
100 Church of St. Vincent in the
   Monastery
101 Church of St. Stephen
102 Church of Our Lady of
   Paradise
103 Church of St. Michael
104 Church of St. Peter
105 Church of St. John of the
   Square
106 Church of St. Sebastian of the
   Bakery
107 Church of the Martyrs
108 Church of St. Paul
109 Church of Our Lady of Hope
   in the Convent of Virgins
110 Church of Our Lady of Loreto
111 Church of the Trinity in the
   Monastery
112 Church of Our Lady of the
   Stairway
113 Church of St. Augustine in
   the Monastery
114 Church of God's Faithful
115 Church of St. Catherine
116 Church of Christ's Wounds
116* Church of Our Lady of
   Victory

OTHER CHURCHES OR CHAPELS

117 Chapel of Our Lady
118 Chapel of the Holy Body
119 Chapel of St. Thomas
120 Chapel of Our Lady of the
   Olives
121 Chapel of Our Lady of Conso-
   lation, above the Gate of Iron

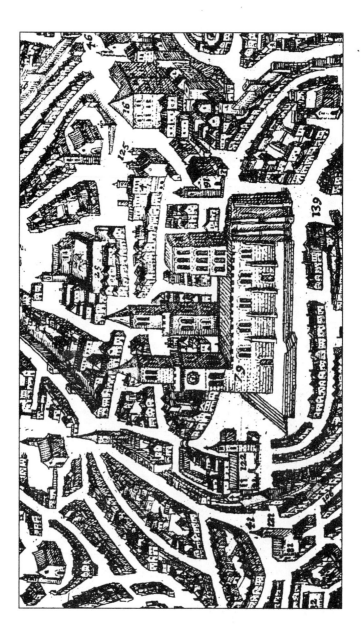

Description of
the City of Lisbon

by the
Portuguese Gentleman
Damião de Góis

To the Renowned Prince Henrique of Portugal,
Most Worthy Titular Cardinal
of the church of SS. Quattro Coronati[1]
of the Most Holy Roman Church,

Damião de Góis, Portuguese Gentleman
S.P.D.

PROLOGUE

Long pressured by the letters of cultivated men urgently
requesting that the history of the affairs of India be brought
to light, I had initially begun to gather documents and sort
through them. The long and restful period of writing that
I enjoyed at the time, without the worries of business matters, permitted me to put my plan into action.

But I then began to consider that perhaps I was lacking
what is so especially required for the writing of history,
and gave up the project. For in truth, whoever intends to
write a complete and impartial history must first secure a
long period of free time; next, he needs peace of mind and
leave of all other activities; and finally, he must benefit from
the favors of the most influential princes, to encourage and
reward his skills and research endeavors.

1

Indeed, at the time I could not abandon other cares and concerns. Consequently, I decided to set aside and apply to this task only the hours available here and there throughout the day, instead of a long, unbroken period of time, as planned. I moved forward, then, with my ongoing projects; and it is only now that I have resolved to undertake the description of the city of Lisbon. And it is only backed by the name of Your Highness that I ventured to publish it, for the use of those who (I repeat) never ceased demanding it.

In this description of Lisbon, I have attempted to paint with the most delicate brush possible all that I was able to uncover regarding the origin of the city proper and its beauty.

Whatever may be the quality and value of this work, I deliberately decided to place it under the protection of Your Highness. Thus, whatever is found wanting in this publication – and certainly I have left many points unresolved – it will still be afforded the comfort and protection of Your Highness's lofty spirit and eminent wisdom. Needing no other shelter, it can safely defend itself from those given to picking at and slandering the works of others.

Greetings!

BOOK I
HISTORY AND ENVIRONS

LISBON AND SEVILLE,
QUEENS OF THE OCEANS

There are two cities that, in this era of ours, we could rightfully call ladies and even Queens of the Sea. For it is under their direction and sovereignty today that navigation is carried out in all of the Orient and Occident.

One of them is Lisbon, which claims for itself dominion over that part of the Ocean that extends from the mouth of the Tagus, to Africa and Asia along an immense maritime circuit. The other is Seville, which, thrusting west from the Guadalquivir River, likewise opened to navigation that part of the globe known today as the New World.

The description of all the feats of this second city I leave to those who will describe the discovery of the New World, and whose writings will no doubt bequeath many memorable things to history.[2]

THE DISCOVERY OF THE
MARITIME ROUTE TO INDIA

Since my purpose is to write only about the circumstances and current state of the city of Lisbon, it seems appropriate that, before attacking the subject, we begin with the event that has made what I am going to write about even more glorious. I refer to the discovery of the maritime passage to India, realized by the Portuguese.

This deed, memorable as it is, will in itself justify my lingering a bit upon it; and, grounded in the testimony of the ancients and in my own research, it may even serve to show the reader how great the difficulties always were to those who, in one way or another, dared attempt an enterprise so fraught with risk.

Let us take as our point of departure the one who, with the greatest willpower and strength of spirit, threw himself into an undertaking so noble for our times. He was the unvanquished son of Dom Afonso V, the glorious king of Portugal, Dom João II.[3] It was he who through war consolidated the kingdom for his people, and through peace reestablished for himself the troubled inheritance of this kingdom.

Then an obsession with events in the Indies took hold of the king's tireless heart with a growing passion. This led him not only to resolve to send exploratory voyages eastward into Indian waters beyond the Ethiopian coast already crossed by the Portuguese, but also to take the initiative to search for land routes.[4]

As I have shown in my book *Faith of the Ethiopians*[5] that overland journey was carried out by Portuguese with extraordinary gifts for understanding oriental customs and languages. I also explained, if superficially, that the islands and coasts of the Atlantic and Ethiopian Ocean had long before been discovered and explored by our navigators, upon the initiative and guidance of the most prudent Prince Henrique.[6] Still in the lifetime of Dom João II, and under the enterprise and auspices of that great Portuguese expert of the nautical arts, Bartolomeu Dias, the Portuguese discovered the far tip of that part of the continent that leads straight up to the Mountains of the Moon. Emerging from the Ocean in the Hesperic Gulf and the Prasso Promontory and extending along both sides towards the South Pole through vast stretches of land, this point lies almost at thirty-five degrees.[7]

MARITIME KNOWLEDGE
OF THE ANCIENTS

Of these territories, or rather, of their Fish-eaters and Cannibals, no such knowledge appears to have reached

Ptolemy.[8] Yet Pliny, Mela, Solinus, and Martianus maintain that in ancient times there was indeed word of this sea route, and that it was fully discovered, from the Indies to the Pillars of Hercules,[9] and even civilized by then along every shore. These authors base themselves on information they compiled on Hannibal,[10] king of the Carthaginians, on Eudoxus, and on others, passed down to them through the writers Juba, Artemidorus,[11] Xenophon of Lampsacus, and Cornelius Nepos, who relate personal experience or the accounts of others in asserting the navigability of this sea.[12] Citing witnesses, they even add that when Augustus' son Caius Caesar was in the Gulf of Arabia, the shipwrecked remains of some Hispanic vessels washed up to shore.

In the same vein of thought, that unparalleled researcher of ancient matters, Herodotus, claims the Greeks were certain that the so-called Atlantic Ocean beyond the Pillars of Hercules and the Red Sea were one and the same sea. And elsewhere he says: the Greeks who inhabit the Point hold as fact that the Ocean encircles the land. Grounding himself in the extremely ancient annals of Egypt, this same Herodotus writes elsewhere: Neco, king of the Egyptian people, having given up the deepening of the trench that goes from the Nile to the Gulf of Arabia, sent some Phoenicians to sea with instructions to pass through the Pillars of Hercules, advancing into the Northern Sea and from there sailing to Egypt. Setting sail from the Red Sea, they arrived at the Southern Sea, and crossing the Strait of Hercules, cast anchor in Egypt two years later. In this way (so it is said), the Greeks were the first to have exact knowledge of the African coast.[13]

There are also writings that confirm that, in the time of Xerxes, Sataspes had gone beyond the Promontory or Cape of Africa. However, extremely tired and disheartened by the wearying voyage, he returned to Egypt via the same Pillars of Hercules through which he had entered the

Atlantic.[14] Finally, Strabo cites information from Aristonicus in reporting that Menelaus, mistakenly drawn out beyond Gades, sailed so far that he came upon the Indies.[15]

I will linger no more on this matter, lest this digression become disproportionately long. One thing, however, seems clear and within the grasp of reason: namely, that this long and infinitely dangerous voyage had always captivated the human spirit to such an extent that, once begun or once concluded, nobody dared venture a second time into such an arduous – if not to say monstrous – undertaking.

Nonetheless, through either the unflagging mettle of the Portuguese or through the sharp urgings of "the accursed hunger for gold"[16] this colossal pilgrimage road is today so well-traveled that we consider this voyage of no greater consequence than one made to England or Belgium.[17]

Let us return to our discussion.

THE PORTUGUESE VOYAGES

Upon the unexpected discovery of the Promontory, that same king, João II, gave it the name Cape of Good Hope, as he hoped that it would offer more favorable circumstances for sailing on into the whole of the Indian Ocean.

Braving the many hazards of accidents and storms, the ships whose command the king had conferred upon Bartolomeu Dias doubled the Cape of Good Hope itself (as we already noted) and entered a river that was given the name Infante River. The reason for this name is that the vessel commanded by the Portuguese Lopo Infante was the first to put into harbor at that river.

They decided that to proceed beyond that point offered not the least guarantee of safety, taking into account that, over the vast reaches of sea they had traversed during their long voyage, they had sighted not a single people who made use of ships. To move on, they feared, would carry the risk of not finding the Hindus, an extremely cultivated and most intelligent people by nature, and might, instead, come upon other races and untamed, barbaric lands. These might inflict upon them even graver setbacks than those already experienced along the coasts and in the ports they had already called at. Assessing the situation with as much prudent good sense as their resources permitted, they reversed course and sailed back to Portugal.

I would readily believe that such an event owes more to divine will than to human judgment. It seems that the full and unspoiled glory of triumphing over the Ocean was reserved by obscure fate to the king who would follow. So it is that King João II died in the meanwhile, leaving the undertaking incomplete. And through a series of unexpected circumstances, which was actually quite common at the time, it was Dom Manuel who assumed command of the kingdom. Two years after taking up the reins of government, seeing that the country was stable within and securely at peace abroad and with neighboring kings, he immediately began turning his attention to the venture that his ancestors had initiated with utmost dedication.[18]

So he ordered that three ships be prepared and outfitted. The command of these he gave to Vasco da Gama, a pure and genuine Portuguese, member of the Order of Chivalry. Once all the necessary arrangements for such an extended voyage were put in order, and taking advantage of favorable winds, he set sail from Lisbon on July 8 of the year of Our Lord 1497. Rapidly he put in at India, aided by favorable winds in auspicious conditions, though with tremendous difficulties.

But leaving aside all of these details, and India itself, let us return to the topic at hand.

THE FOUNDING AND NAMING OF LISBON

Who originally founded Lisbon I do not dare say with certainty, from the distance of so many centuries. The most ancient writers include it, however, among the oldest cities in Hispania. Varro calls it *Olisiponem*; Ptolemy,

Oliosiponem[19]; Strabo gives it the name of *Odysseia* and seems to assert, with the words of Asclepiades Mirlianus, that it was founded by Ulysses.[20] This Mirlianus presided over a literary contest in Turdestan and wrote a book about the peoples of the region.[21] He goes so far as to say that in Lisbon there were found, hung from the temple of Minerva, certain objects, such as shields, garlands and spurs, alluding to the voyages of Ulysses.

Some authors, it is true, find this to be insufficient evidence from which to convincingly deduce that Lisbon had been founded by Ulysses. I am more satisfied, however, to agree with the opinion of an illustrious writer such as he than to adopt the ideas of naysayers who scoff at him without any solid argument of their own. Especially as it is true that Solinus, a person of extraordinary culture, shares the viewpoint of the aforementioned Strabo. And even our own André de Resende, an author of reliable judgment in the estimation of all cultivated persons, adopts and confirms the same opinion at many points in his writings.[22]

Returning to the issue of Lisbon's name, we must unhesitatingly conclude, based on an explanation by the aforementioned Resende and on many ancient inscriptions found in the city itself and collected by him, that it is to be written *Olisiponem*, with an "o," two "i"s, and only one "s."

In Roman times, Olisipo was a municipality of Roman citizens. Here I cannot refrain from presenting the contribution of Pliny, a most illustrious writer. Says he: "The municipality of Roman citizens is Lisbon, surnamed the Success of Julius."[23]

And the origin of the name "Olisipo"? For lack of sources, I do not dare take stock in any claim. Perhaps this seems steeped in fable to many, just as a certain phrase by Varro was judged to be by Justin. Varro writes: "In Lusitania, where the city Olisipo is, the mares on Mount Tagro become pregnant through the wind alone." Pliny and Solinus admit this as fact. However, as I said, Justin asserts categorically that such an opinion is erroneous. Here are his words: "Many authors recounted that in Lusitania, along the Tagus River, the mares conceive through the wind alone. Such legends derive from the mares' great fertility and from the quantity of herds: these are so numerous in Galicia and in Lusitania, and they run so speedily, that they seem in fact to have been conceived by the wind itself."[24]

I would not disagree with Justin's explanation as such had not physicians ways to prove that nature is wont to produce and procreate many things through the feminine sex alone, not united with the masculine. And likewise, in his *History* the archbishop of Toledo, Dom Rodrigo, endorses Varro's assertion with a considerable number of arguments.[25]

SINTRA AND COLARES

Regarding the Mount Tagro mentioned by Varro, it is in my opinion one and the same with what we call the Serra de Sintra [Sintra Ridge], and from which the Promontory of the Moon juts out toward the sea, located about twenty-four thousand paces from Lisbon. Nowadays we know this promontory as Cabo da Roca, or *Rupem* in Latin.[26]

Today along the side of this hill can be seen a village endowed with a graceful location and admirably moderate climate. Ennobled with a grand and magnificent palace of the Portuguese kings, it is called Sintra, after the forest. In that forest there is such an abundance of game and fowl, and the special soil is so well-suited for the grazing of livestock, that it is not difficult for anyone to convince himself that the mares conceived without outside intervention.

On a knoll about two-thousand paces from this ridge toward the ocean, rests a village which the locals have named Colares. Not far from the village, below a rocky cliff overhanging the sea, lies a grotto battered by the ocean. The grotto swallows the waves that find their way inside, where they pound against each other in a clash of water and spray, and then it disgorges them with a surging, swelling roar.

And so it is that we believe in a sighting there long ago of a triton singing with his shell.

TRITONS AND MERMAIDS

Insofar as the site is concerned, I do not dare pass judgment with confidence, especially since the locale can easily be seen and scrutinized by anyone who skirts closely along the shoreline. But regarding the triton, Pliny has written that it was seen and heard in Lusitania during the time of Tiberius Caesar. He writes: "An embassy from Lisbon sent for the purpose reported to the Emperor Tiberius that a triton had been seen and heard playing on a shell in a certain cave, and that he had the well-known shape."[27]

And I believe that the following should not go unsaid: in our own times, at various places along the neighboring coastline, a kind of being has been found that the local inhabitants have begun calling by the name of marine-man. This is due to its nature and origin, above all to the fact that on the surface of its skin it still bears certain wrinkles or scales that are spread over almost all of its body, like the vestiges of some ancient race. It has forever been held as truth that these beings owe their origin and ascendancy to the marine-men, or tritons.

According to the beliefs of our ancestors, all of this arises from the way tritons used to jump onto land, little by little becoming accustomed to playing on the beach. Attracted by the sweetness of the fruit, which in that region is quite abundant, they returned there often. Through the supreme cunning of the inhabitants, some of these were caught and later introduced with affection to a more civilized, less wild, form of life.[28]

Might it seem pure fantasy to anyone that the tritons, through close dealings with people, managed to utter articulated sounds? And that they even shared contact with the Lusitanians at all? Well, to me it would seem far more fantastic for a wild and uncouth triton to have jumped from Lake Triton, in Africa,[29] and, amusing himself with the Greeks, to have asked Jason to give him the stool he was carrying to Delphi, so as to avoid the hazardous reefs!

To inject a more convincing witness into the debate, let me refer to the fisherman of our own times who went to try his luck with hook and line among the boulders of the Bárbaro Promontório [Cabo Espichel], near the Hermitage of Santa Maria.[30] Suddenly there leapt from the waves onto these rocks a male triton with flowing beard, long hair, wrinkled chest, a face not terribly disfigured, and perfectly human features. Having remained a while to bask in the sun and steal sidelong glances at the man, who returned the attention, he suddenly took fright and, crying out in a voice almost human, plunged back into the sea. The fisherman still recounts this story today to whomever will hear it, describing the triton, or marine-man, with great detail and fine words.

Here is yet another report, an incident that took place only a few years ago not far from the Promontory of the Moon. Fernão Alvares, notary of the India House and a completely trustworthy man, had a small piece of land in the countryside near the Promontory of the Moon, with a serious and credible peasant for his neighbor. This notary told me that the neighbor often headed out to some rocks along the beach to fish. Now on one day of particularly good fishing – just as Fernão Alvares heard it from the source! – upon catching each fish he would toss it into a dry hollow in the rock behind him, for safekeeping. This he repeated several times, until he noticed the presence among the rocks of a naked and beardless young boy. He paid no mind, thinking that it was one of the inhabitants from the outskirts who often went swimming in the area. To this lad he directed not a word, amused as he was with his fishing. But then, looking more carefully, he watched as the boy grabbed each fish, took it to his mouth and ate it! Enraged, the fisherman ran to catch the boy, but the latter fled in a fit of laughter, prancing up to the edge of the rock and springing lightly into the ocean.

Almost at the same time, across the river on the other side of the city and not far from the village that we call Barreiro,[31] the sea flung onto the beach near the country home of the nobleman Afonso de Albuquerque a marineman of the same appearance, but dead.

Moreover, in the ancient archives of the kingdom [the Torre do Tombo], the highest command of which I personally hold, there is a most ancient manuscript of a contract carried out between King Afonso III and Paio Peres, master of the Order of the Knights of Santiago. In that document it is ordered that the tax on mermaids and other sorts of animals fished from the beaches of the aforementioned order be paid to the king and queen, and not to the master of the order. From which it is obviously deduced that the mermaids were plentiful in our waters at the time, since a law concerning them was promulgated.

But enough of tritons, nymphs, and mermaids.

Ancient History of Lisbon

Let us return, then, to the matter at hand. It must be kept in mind – as we said a little earlier – that nothing is known for sure about the origin and reason behind the name of the city of Lisbon. Moreover, neither Greek nor Latin authors offer any verification regarding its ancient history, nor about the happenings there in times gone by. And yet, in a city where today one can find so many stones inscribed with high praises and epitaphs in Latin, there is not the slightest doubt that ancient times also saw many

splendid events with which we could embellish and il-
lustrate this narrative of ours.

It is only reasonable to suppose that all of those things
surely disappeared more through the wear and tear of time
than through the disregard of writers. Thus we will only
begin our account with the Portuguese *Annals*, since we
do not dare include anything resembling legend. We will
explain how, after the grievous disaster in which nearly
all of Hispania abandoned the Christian faith under
Moorish rule, the city of Lisbon also returned to Christ.
These things happened in the following way.[32]

THE CHRISTIAN RECONQUEST

Because the Moors had made repeated raids into Hispania
since long ago, devout Christian men from everywhere
came to her aid, lending support to their king and queen.
So it happened that, among others, the count of Toledo,
Dom Raimundo [also of Burgundy], came to the rescue of
King Alfonso of Castille,[33] emperor-elect. With him he
brought on this expedition Count Dom Henrique [of Bur-
gundy], faithful companion and son of his sister.

There is disagreement among authors regarding the
birthplace of Dom Henrique. Castillian writers say that
he was born in Constantinople; the French guarantee that
he was from Lorraine; our own look to Hungary for his
origins. However, neither one nor another proves his assertions with the solid reasoning that would allow us to form
a firm opinion.

What is certain is that, due to the extraordinary merits
of these leaders, King Alfonso of Castille gave his daugh-
ters in marriage to them: to Raimundo, Urraca; to
Henrique, Teresa.[34] Furthermore, as dowry he turned over
to Henrique and Teresa the county of Portugal, a province
largely under Moorish domain at the time.

AFONSO HENRIQUES, THE PORTUGUESE NATION, AND THE FLAG

From Teresa, Henrique had one son, Afonso. After many famous deeds practiced on behalf of the Christian faith, and having defeated in a single battle five mighty Moorish kings at Campos de Ourique, near Castro Verde,[35] this Afonso was simultaneously elected, acclaimed, and sworn in as king by the soldiers on the very site of their encampment. Though he put up resistance, all were joined together as one, tirelessly protesting that it was unacceptable for such spirited soldiers as themselves to wage harrowing battle against famous monarchs unless under the standard of a king.

Our own writers recount that, before entering battle, this same Afonso saw Christ in the skies, nailed to the cross and promising him victory. The king, inflamed with faith, responded with these words: "Lord, it is not necessary that you appear before me, for I firmly believe that you are the Son of God and the true Savior of the world. Go, then, and show yourself to the enemies of your religion, so that we may be spared great misfortune, and so they may come to believe that it is only through your death that the world has life and salvation."

In memory of this miracle, Afonso ordered that upon his shield, which was only white until then, there be carved five smaller blue shields, signifying the five defeated kings. And in each of these smaller shields he arranged five white points – four corners with a center – recalling Christ's wounds. Ever since that time, the kings of Portugal use those symbols with the greatest of veneration, kissing them and keeping safe their memory with all due honor, because of their glorious mysteries. There is one other mysterious aspect to these signs, worthy of being made known: it is that, by adding the number of all the white points to those five little shields the number thirty is obtained; that is, thirty coins, the price at which Judas sold Christ, Savior of the world, to the Jews.

This is why the kings of Portugal adopted, after that remarkable victory, such glorious and significant symbols as these. And just as these signs were granted from the high heavens by Christ, so we, fighting on beneath their guidance, spread the faith of Christ today throughout the vast universe, extending it with our active efforts more widely and effectively than it had ever been before.

THE TAKING OF LISBON FROM THE MOORS

Let us return to the topic.

Surrounded by the said King Afonso and besieged during a long and hard war, Lisbon was finally restored to the Christian faith in the year of Christ's birth 1147. Some crusaders also took part in this war, coming from various regions of Europe to defend the faith. Not a few died in combat.[36]

Nor were there lacking those whose accounts of miracles brought them sainthood. Among them figures a German named Henrique, a native of Bonn (which is a settlement established along the banks of the Rhine, not far from Colonia Agrippina [Cologne]). Due to the special merits of this Henrique, God saw fit to work many amazing miracles, as our *Annals* attest.[37]

RELICS OF SAINT VINCENT AND THE SÉ CATHEDRAL

In the reign of this King Afonso, some time after the siege and conquest of the Moors at Lisbon, the body of the deacon and martyr Saint Vincent was transported from the Promontório Sacro, where it had been hidden for many years, to the city proper of Lisbon. Placed in the arch of the great cathedral [the Sé], it is venerated today with deep devotion.[38] Our own Resende devoted a solemn and lengthy poem to this subject.[39]

In front of this monument is found the sepulchre of King Afonso IV, who in the year of Our Lord 1340 valiantly came to the aid of his son-in-law Afonso, king of Castile, against the mighty Moorish king Alboacem. He was the leader of the armies who waged bloody battle along the Salado River against the said Alboacem, achieving glorious victory and causing the people to hail him as the Victor of Salado.[40] This is the reason that gives me the pleasure to set in relief this mention of the king.

CHAPEL OF SAINT ANTHONY

Near the entranceway of this important cathedral [the Sé], a little down to the west and separated from it by a square, we come upon the Chapel of Saint Anthony of Padua [Santo António de Padua], as he is popularly known. It is a work of admirable construction and wonderful elegance, home in previous times to the parents of this Saint Anthony, and where he was born and raised. The city of Lisbon takes great pride in being the cradle of this saint, and rightfully so, as he was included in the roll and catalog of the saints, with unanimous Christian acclaim. Affirming popular Christian opinion with the seal of miracles, God let the name of Saint Anthony become known throughout the entire world, and his memory honored and proclaimed everywhere by all people.[41]

Over the epistilio[42] of this chapel is housed the municipal seat, or curia, about whose organization and regime we could recount many important things, if that were not outside the range of our topic. Let us return, therefore, to what we have begun to do.

THE TAGUS ESTUARY

In early times the site of ancient Lisbon occupied only one high hill that extended down to the bank of the Tagus. Nowadays its scope encompasses several hills and valleys.

The most important and famous area faces east. At this most important part the sea receives the waters of the Tagus, then opens up into an estuary six-thousand paces wide.[43]

THE OTHER SIDE OF THE TAGUS

The opposite shoreline forms two bays: one, pushing inland and toward the north, leads to a land known as Aldeia Galega, which is today rather well-settled; the other, turning slightly southward, allows for daily sailings to the village of Coina.[44]

A bit further downstream on this side lies the fortress of Almada, at the extreme tip of the sweeping curve of Coina's bay. At this point, then, the sea looks in upon a slight narrowing of the inlet. The distance from there to the city is a little less than four-thousand paces.[45] The bank of that side falls almost vertically to the sea and, wheeling south like an arch, extends out to the Promontório Bárbaro [Cabo Espichel].

Among the cliffs on this side of the river are nestled inaccessible stretches of winding shoreline, like a series of shoals. Here is where our contemporaries go prospecting for gold mixed with sand, namely in the place they call Adiça; however, gold is also found in several other places along the banks of the Tagus. This is, furthermore, in agreement with the claims of ancient authors who wrote that the Tagus was rich in gold and precious stones.[46]

UP THE RIGHT BANK OF THE TAGUS

Crossing back from the Promontório Bárbaro to this side of the Tagus, the Promontory of the Moon [Cabo da Roca] advances toward the ocean, facing west and marking the beginning of the territory of the ancient Túrdulos.[47] We came to call this place the Old Beach and continue to do so today.

Going inland a short distance from the widest point in the opening of the Lisbon estuary a hermitage dedicated to the Virgin Mary and called Our Lady the Guide [Nossa Senhora da Guia] can be seen over the cliffs. Beacons are lit there at night to show the way to navigators, who, not knowing those places well, thereby avoid having their ships dragged in and hurled against the reefs and outlying boulders.

Coasting upland from there to the north one comes upon the fortress of Cascais,[48] in whose wide and sheltered port cargo vessels set anchor to await favorable tides and winds. A short distance further up the river an elbow-shaped bay is formed, with the Hermitage of São Julião[49] at its far end. And further upstream is another dedicated to Saint Catherine [Santa Catarina].

BOOK II
AROUND THE CITY WALLS, FROM BELÉM TO THE GATE OF THE CROSS

BELÉM

So, moving nearer the city along the same side of the river you reach the stronghold of Belém,[50] just in from the beach.

And there we come upon a grand cathedral [the Jerónimos][51] dedicated to the Most Holy Virgin, together with a monastery of monks who take the vows of the order of Saint Jerome. It is an incredibly sumptuous and magnificent building, envisioned by the glorious King Manuel himself as his mausoleum, and ordered built by him while still alive. However, it was João III, son of King Manuel and happily our ruler now, who ordered the expansion of the monument, which is still underway.

In this regard, on an arch there can be read a celebrated quatrain set in large lettering by our own Resende, which I am not averse to citing, as visiting foreigners frequently take note of it:

VASTA MOLE SACRVM DIVINAE IN LITORE MATRI
REX POSVIT REGVM MAXIMVS EMMANVEL.
AVXIT OPVS HAERES REGNI ET PETATIS: VTERQVE
STRVCTVRA CERTANT, RELIGIONE PARES.[52]

In front of this house of worship rises a tower [the Torre de Belém] of four floors, constructed of carved stone. This structure, also undertaken by the aforementioned King Manuel, was built above the rocks scattered in the sea, so that it was completely surrounded by water and impervious to any unexpected assault or enemy attack. And, due to the narrowness of the passage, it was impossible for any ships to manage an approach to the city without the consent of those standing guard in the tower.[53]

From here to the outermost extremity of the city there is a distance of about three-thousand paces.[54] All along this stretch one can observe a number of suburban villas, constructed with admirable elegance and delight. One also sees fields and pasturelands, as well as an extraordinary abundance of all kinds of fruit, which at a mere glance betray great beauty and stir the appetite.[55]

SANTOS-O-VELHO TO SÃO ROQUE

If I intended to describe every one of the things found within the bounds of the city, that would drag out far too long. Therefore, let us not stray from the proposed purpose.

The beginning of the city of Lisbon along this southern edge[56] is marked by the Old Palace [Santos-o-Velho], which we call "of Santos," a huge, magnificent, and very beautiful structure. The name was given to the place by the fact that for ages the bodies of the martyred saints Veríssimo, Máxima, and Júlia were kept there, until being transferred to another locale during the reign of King João II. For having proclaimed their faith in Christ as the Son of God and Savior of the world, these saints were executed by order of the Roman prefect.[57]

From here, along a tortuous, stone-paved road with a slow, downward grade, one comes upon the convent of nuns known as Santa Maria da Esperança. From here, this road rises up to the bordering hill, on whose opposite slope is seen the chapel called São Roque.[58]

FROM SÃO ROQUE TO OUR LADY OF THE MOUNT

Following this same route, one descends into a most agreeable valley, contiguous to the city walls and full of orchards and gardens.[59] In earlier times it took on the name of a chapel of hermits dedicated to Saint Anthony. As the hermits since left there, however, it now bears the name of the

Annunciation [the Anunciada] by the Angel to the Virgin Mother of God and is inhabited by the nuns of the Dominican Order.[60]

From here, along a parallel, downward slope, emerges a hill that is so densely covered with olive trees that it is difficult to see inside it. It is open, however, on the highest part, and was beautified recently with the chapel dedicated to Saint Ann [Santa Ana], which is frequented nowadays by everyone. Many devotees flock there to worship because of the great piety and veneration observed in the services.

From here, by way of a pasture field and, lying further inside, a lepers' hospital and cattle market, one arrives at another valley, no less fertile and pleasant. It is called the Mouraria, since it was there that the Moors were given permission to live after the city was taken back from the Saracens.[61] The Chapel of the Angels [Igreja dos Anjos] divides the left-hand part of the valley toward the north, where the fields of Santa Barbara begin. Above this valley toward the east rises up a high hill with a steep and difficult incline, for which the temple on the summit, Our Lady of the Mount [Nossa Senhora do Monte], was named.[62]

FROM GRAÇA DOWN TO THE RIVERBANK

Leaving this place one takes a slight turn and then follows a nearly straight line back to the city. Immediately appearing now is the most ancient temple of the Augustinian monks, dedicated to Our Lady of Grace [Nossa Senhora da Graça][63] and set against the city walls along its inside edge. In passing we can note the great riches of the monastery of the canons of Saint Augustine, dedicated to the deacon and martyr Saint Vincent [São Vicente de Fora],[64] and the Ginásio [the Escolas Gerais], which had not been so famous before King João III transferred it to Coimbra. From here, then, one comes upon the bank of the Tagus, which marks the northernmost point of the city.

In this area the vast and most noble monastery of the nuns of Santa Clara [Convento de Santa Clara] almost reaches the riverbank. Taking the opposite direction and leaving aside the Chapel of Our Lady of Paradise [Nossa Senhora do Paraíso], one gains access to the first of the city gates, the so-called Gate of the Cross [Porta da Cruz].

Overall Appearance

From the temple of Santa Clara back to the Old Royal Palace, which we said is called Santos, and which is located at the far south of the city on the right bank, the distance moving along the sea from the east toward the south measures about three-thousand paces.[65] This side of the city, then, is bathed by the sea, while the other three sides have access by land.

As a result, with its five hills[66] and many other extremely fertile and very delightful valleys, the city encompasses a space whose perimeter may be calculated at seven-thousand paces.[67] It does not strike me as very easy, however, to make an exact drawing and description of Lisbon, seeing as how it is settled on uneven, mountainous terrain. Nonetheless, if one were to look out upon Lisbon, observing its placement and overall aspect within the global, panoramic view had from the Castle of Almada – which we have already noted to be on the other side of the estuary – it would no doubt be verified that the shape of the city resembles that of a fish bladder. If the ground were entirely flat it would appear from that side to have the form of an arch.

The City Center

As far as the city center is concerned, its grandeur and magnificence are such that it stands up to any other European city, as much for the number of inhabitants as for the beauty and variety of its buildings. Indeed, the houses are said to number over twenty-thousand.[68]

Whether of royal and noble families or of simple, private owners, a large percentage of these houses are built with truly unbelievable elegance and splendor; to such a degree that the inside walls and arcades are completely clad in Sarmatian[69] woods and embellished with gilt carvings and multicolored paintings.

Springs and Fountains

Many springs issue forth along the shoreline, with underground channels from various points in the city that supply the population with water.

One of these is called the King's Fountain [Chafariz d'El Rei], a remarkable structure with columns and marble archwork. So much water gushes forth from its six spouts that it alone could provide for the drinking needs of everyone. Due to the water's high level of purity, its flavor, and lightness, this fountain equals or betters all the others I can remember having seen. The water streams out lukewarm, but after settling for a short period of time it takes on a great purity and freshness, so that it is a pleasure to drink.

Nearby, two more springs shoot forth great torrents of water, which run down to the sea like a brook. If they were a greater distance from the sea, many watermills could easily be turned – in any season of the year – by the intensity and force of this current. At the very least they are of great use to the washerwomen and the hide tanners and dressers.[70]

At a relatively short distance toward the Gate of the Cross there appears another spring, or rather a tank, which is known as the Fountain of the Horses [Chafariz dos Cavalos or "Chafariz de Dentro"] because of the sculpted horses whose muzzles shoot jets of water, which in turn flow out of the tank in small streams.

In still other places within the city there are numerous springs and wells with a variety of waters, accruing greatly to the well-being of the citizens. To list all of them one by one at this point would not seem to be of much interest here.[71]

BOOK III
SEVEN MAGNIFICENT
BUILDINGS

Let us make a brief and concise pass through other monuments adorning the city.

Leaving aside the Old Palace of the King – a structure that neatly reflects the very image of antiquity, situated high on the citadel, which itself occupies the highest point of the city[72] – we can say that the Lisbon of our times is aggrandized principally by virtue of seven splendid buildings of incredible sumptuousness, magnanimously constructed with the singular wisdom of our enlightened kings.[73]

The First Building:
The Church of the Misericórdia

To begin with religion, the first among these buildings is the Church of the Misericórdia [Igreja da Misericórdia],[74] elegantly constructed throughout with custom-fitted stonework. It is sustained not through elevated rental incomes, nor through perpetual annuities, as is the case with the majority of our royal institutions today. Rather, it is through the forthcoming contributions of generous nobles and pious individuals, so that only with difficulty can one believe how much money is spent each year on the poor.

The caretakers of this home call themselves associates, or, more strictly speaking, Brothers of Mercy. Management is entrusted to them, due as much to the nobility of their name and lineage as to the prestige of their honesty and religious character. Jointly and of a single mind they administer the Church of the Misericórdia's funds, which are gathered up only from the offerings of pious contributors and from alms. Acting without discrimination and proceeding with the utmost integrity and loyalty, they come to the aid of the needy, attending especially the orphan girls. To these are allotted dowries, corresponding to the possibilities of each. Aid is likewise offered to those who, struck by misfortune or unhappiness, are forced to bear the burden of a life of sadness and hardship.

Year after year the unfailing accuracy and absence of corruption in the distribution of these monies to the poor prompts ever greater generosity from many people, both our compatriots and foreigners alike. The Church of the Misericórdia cannot continue dispensing a donation for more than a year, nor does it make profits, as per the customs and statutes of its order. In this light, it is yet more admirable that more than twenty-four-thousand gold ducats are distributed to the poor each year. And there were even some years in which the sum of forty-thousand ducats was attained.

THE SECOND BUILDING: THE ALL-SAINTS HOSPITAL

Following in second place is another example of mercy and humanity, that is, a public sanatorium for the poor and sick called the All-Saints Hospital [Hospital de Todos-os-Santos].[75]

In no way does it suffer in comparison to the previously-mentioned building, not for the magnificence of its facilities, not for its total expenditures, not even for the care with which they treat the poor – afflicted with various bodily ailments – and take in waifs to be fed and educated.

The building is divided into four cloisters with very delightful gardens. It has thirty-four arched vaults all the way around, each of which leads to magnificent chambers filled with dining halls and dormitories, the latter conveniently provided with beds and the cleanest of linen.

The poor patients are received here with care and generosity and are not permitted to leave until their health has been completely restored. Upon leaving, some are even given a small sum of money, enough to live on for a few days without work or hardship, until they find themselves completely recovered.

Alongside the hospital are some houses, or quarters, for various types of employees: treasurers, solicitors, doctors, pharmacists, and other officials. This way, in case of emergency or need, they are always available to minister to the sick, by day or night, with diligence and speed.

To summarize: everything is done in such a way that our hospital can justly claim primacy among all royal hospitals found throughout Spain or the other parts of the Christian world, however numerous and renowned they be.

In front of the entrance gate at this hospital stretches a vast plaza or field [Rossio],[76] squared off all around by a series of lovely buildings, from which the above-mentioned valleys of Santo Antão and the Mouraria commence. Together these valleys take on the shape of the letter "delta" as they flow out toward the sea, rolling across different lands and resembling an oxhide without the tail.[77]

To the right of the hospital, from north to west, are located the Church of São Domingos [Igreja de São Domingos] and a highly regarded academy [Colegio de Santo Antão or Coleginho].

THE THIRD BUILDING: THE ESTAUS PALACE

Crossing westward to the opposite face of the Rossio, the third monument rises up. A truly magnificent building, the Estaus Palace [Paço dos Estaus][78] deserves to be seen for its admirable architecture, which Prince Pedro, son of King João I, ordered built with the nation's treasuries while regent of the kingdom in the name of King Afonso V, his nephew on the side of his father. In ordering it erected there his only intention was to offer lodging to ambassadors of foreign nations and their kings, who were received there at public expense with all high pomp and honors.[79]

Following a straight line toward the shoreline, we pass along the right, and higher up, the convents of the Carmelites [Carmo],[80] of the Franciscans [São Francisco], and of the Order of the Trinity [Trindade], all of them most noteworthy for the beauty and richness of their architecture.

We move now through the Rua Nova d'El-Rei, replete with engravers, jewelers, gem-cutters, silversmiths, goldsmiths, goldplaters, and moneychangers. And bearing continually to the left one arrives at another "new" street, the Rua Nova dos Mercadores,[81] much wider than the others and adorned on both sides with exquisite buildings. Every day merchants representing almost every people and region of the world flock together here, joined by great throngs of people enjoying the advantages of business at the port.

Advancing through the same street toward the north, one comes upon the old tax office on the left-hand side. Until recently it was here that duties owed on imported merchandise were paid to the king.

In front of this office appears a plaza called the Old Pillory [Pelourinho Velho]. Seated before tables in this plaza can always be seen many men who might be called notaries or scribes, although they have no official duties. All of them make a living through the following process: listening attentively to those who come to lay out their problems before them, they immediately write onto sheets of paper that are then given over to the client, who pays according to the services rendered. So they are always at hand there, ready to compose letters, amorous messages, eulogies, speeches, epitaphs, verses, encomiums, funeral prayers, petitions, notes and other things of this kind that are asked of them. Never have I seen anything like this in any other city of Europe.[82]

Around here one can easily appreciate the grandeur of Lisbon and the number of its inhabitants.[83]

The Fourth Building:
The Public Granary

From here there is a straight street leading to the Church of the Misericórdia, about which we have already spoken. Adjoining the vestibule of this church on the east side is the fourth building [Terreiro do Trigo, the Granary], certainly earning eternal memory for King João III. This is a structure with two wings, magnificent subdivisions, many additional galleries and thirty-two arches on both sides, and endowed with eighty storage rooms and a flat, narrow patio in the center. It can justifiably be called the granary of the nation and the pantry of Lusitania.

That public granary was established there by the magnificent and prudent king, with the aim of abolishing the tax on wheat and other cereals and vegetables (he was the first king of Portugal to make this concession to the people, at huge cost to the treasury). It was hoped that the enhanced profits thereby afforded to the merchants would motivate them to search out wheat anywhere it could be found and bring it back there.

This plan quickly relieved the needs of the people, which in turn accrued to the great advantage of the nation, as we witnessed not long ago.

The Fifth Building:
The New Custom House

That building stands back-to-back with the New Custom House [Alfândega Nova], which extends right up to the edge of the sea. It is a tremendous mass of rock, underpinned by huge, closely spaced pylons hammered into the sea, and constructed upon the order and expense of this same king. Mindful of the magnificence of these facilities and their beautiful construction, I rightfully felt obliged to accord it the fifth place in this series.

Continuing along the same road in the direction of the river's current, one comes upon a wide field that begins at the new custom house and granary, bounded on the north and west with exquisite buildings. Along the south there is a noteworthy colonnade, quite ornate and most agreeable in appearance, which extends down to the shoreline. The other side of the field, facing east, is bordered by the sea.[84]

In this square are found the facilities of the fish- and sweet-markets. Every day crowds of fishmongers, green-grocers, confectioners, butchers, bakers, and candymakers converge there, selling everything they bring to feed the city. Stalls of shopkeepers, innkeepers, and weavers can also be seen, well-stocked with foods and wines.[85]

In the fishmarket there is a great quantity of baskets, placed there at the behest of the authorities, in which the fish is transported by cargo boys to women fishmongers of the plaza, before the ships have even tied up. These baskets are on yearly lease to the fishermen by the public authorities, at a cost of two-thousand ducats. In this respect I confess to feeling undecided and perplexed over whether I should congratulate the city for augmenting its income in this way, or if I should condemn that form of veiled tyranny.

But I have not brought up this matter except to show foreigners the opulence of the city.[86]

THE SIXTH BUILDING: THE CEUTA HOUSE AND THE INDIA HOUSE

Leaving aside the aforementioned fish plaza, and passing up the market of bakers, of fruit and vegetable vendors, the market for fowl, and the plaza of foodstuffs, in the western corner of this square is located a building that we call the Ceuta House [Casa de Ceuta], where the royal commissioners dispatch matters concerned with the war in Africa.[87]

In a contiguous row of buildings not far from this house rises the sixth monument, executed in marvelous style and replete with the abundant spoils and plunderings from many nations and peoples. Because it is there where the business affairs with India are handled, our people have named it the India House [Casa da Índia]. In my opinion, it might sooner be called an opulent emporium, due to its aromas, pearls, rubies, emeralds, and other precious stones brought to us from India year after year; or perhaps a grand depository of gold and silver, whether in bars or fashioned into forms. There stand patent, for whoever wishes to admire them, innumerable compartments arranged with an artful cleverness, overflowing with such a great abundance of those treasures that – word of honor! – it would surpass one's capacity to believe, if they did not leap before the eyes of all, and if we could not touch them with our own hands.

From the high end of the grand and sumptuous Royal Palace [Paços da Ribeira], which King Manuel had ordered built for himself, an immense colonnade advances toward the sea like a war machine, marking the southern edge of the square to which we have already alluded. At the far end of the colonnade a skillfully carved stone tower rises up over the beach, facing east.[88]

Just next to that, right up along the shoreline of the river, our mighty lord King João III recently began to raise from the foundations another building of admirable features. When it is finished, with the aid of God and his saints, it will occupy the eighth place among the beauties of the city, stealing the show, no doubt, from all the other monuments.

THE SEVENTH BUILDING: THE WAR ARMORY

Finally, near the Royal Palace, which (as I said) was built by King Manuel, on the opposite side of this new building, toward the west and separated by a plaza along the inside, one can find the seventh and last public monument. It is endowed with a great number of subdivisions and wings on all sides, elaborately adorned with art. So many are the entrances and so diverse the exits within the interior compartments that it could indeed be considered a genuine labyrinth.

Here our kings established the War Armory [Arsenal de Guerra],[89] replete with vast numbers of every sort of weapon, war machine, mortar, and everything else pertaining to the conduct of war by land and by sea; and the quantity is such that, whether in terms of war machines or in terms of the infinite number of arms and spears, it easily surpasses all other arsenals – however well equipped and fully stocked – found today throughout Europe and Asia, most of which I have visited.[90]

I believe it may be easier for me to prove this, no matter to whom, with the following argument: for routine naval expeditions alone, the king is obliged to maintain in Asia, Africa, and Europe more than two-hundred ships of all types, their munitions, and equipment in permanent, impeccable readiness.

Stored with the greatest vigilance and cleanliness in three halls of this building are forty-thousand suits of armor for the infantry, plus three-thousand complete sets for the cavalry, beyond those destined for use in routine or extraordinary exercises. Also kept here are the most varied pieces of artillery: mortars, scorpions [missile-launchers for defense of city walls], basilisks [large brass cannons], lions [small artillery], creese [long-range artillery], camels [machines for adding buoyancy to vessels], trebuchets [heavy missile-launchers], dispersers, cannon of uncommon size and weight, as well as other better-known assault weapons that people call falcons [light cannons], cradles [support structures for ships under repair], and muskets. And there is powder and bullets of stone and iron in such great abundance that if I tried to detail and describe the various kinds, the number, and weight of each, I fear that I might be seen as setting forth untruths in this text instead of real facts. Therefore, content yourselves with reading or hearing only what I have already described.

So let us return now to what remains ahead.

BOOK IV
ADDITIONAL INFORMATION

As I mentioned earlier, that part of the city bathed by the sea boasts twenty-two gates, it being the most dignified of areas. The part facing land has sixteen gates. And every one of these is indispensable, due to the city's immense number of inhabitants and the great extent of its perimeter. It is defended by seventy-seven towers set along the course of the city battlements.

The churches in which the sacraments are administered to all the faithful, known by the Greek name of *paroikos* [parish], number twenty-five, not counting the many other houses of worship entrusted to monks, friars, and nuns.

In praise of religious music I will add here an absolutely authentic fact known perfectly well to all the city dwellers: on the year's principal feast days, more than thirty complete choral groups file out of the city to chant the religious solemnities through the surrounding towns and villages. And although they all leave the city together on the same day, none of the city's various houses of worship where music is chanted suffers in any way through the celebration of these festivities.[91]

There are one-hundred-thirty-one of these associations, known to us as brotherhoods. A considerable sum of money is collected each year from the societies' brothers for their works; it is then distributed under the most rigorous standards to the poor, and used also for other necessary expenses.

Regarding the healthfulness of Lisbon and its location, as well as the mildness of its climate, there is such a gentle and agreeable harmony between the land and atmosphere that on almost no day of the year will one feel excessive heat or cold. Attracted, then, by the purity of the climate, many foreigners from a variety of nations and far-off regions immigrate here, abandoning their native turf and the cares of their homeland to take up lifelong residence here.

Scanning the city's outlying lands in any direction, one finds them to be sprinkled with magnificent country houses and rustic farms, owing to the fecundity of the fields and the great density of inhabitants. And many people even prefer to live in the country over the city, for the continual prosperity of all things there and because of the profound peace long enjoyed among the community.

And it is a spiritual treat to contemplate the fields, which are not only densely settled with villages and country homes, but also splashed with numerous, well-endowed churches and convents. The surrounding country homes and rustic farmhouses exceed six-hundred in number.[92]

There are two-hundred-and-forty villages under the jurisdiction of the city magistrate. Among them, thirty-six retain their own judges and tribunals, enjoying the right to administer justice to the inhabitants, to judge litigants, and settle disputes among the villagers. But if the suit involves a capital offense, recourse is sought from the supreme magistrate of the city, who is required to return a sentence.

Up the Tagus to Santarém

Finally, to encompass in a brief epilogue everything that might add to the aggrandizement of the city's image, I will say that about fifty miles upstream from Lisbon, along one side of the Tagus, is situated the city of Scallabis. It is very old and quite famous among the many Lusitanian cities. Pliny asserts that it was the fifth colony of Lusitania, known in other days as "Praesidium Julium."[93] Today we call it Santarém. Lovers of ancient history will find abundant information about this in the works of our own Resende.

Sitting on the summit of a high hill, the city looks far and wide over an extensive plain – divided along the middle by the Tagus – where the land surpasses all others in fertility. With only light cultivation on small plots it annually produces incredible quantities of wheat. To give an idea of the soil's fertility, I will not shrink from adding (what to many will seem difficult to believe) that sixty days after the sowing of seed, the tilled lands are mature and harvested, the wheat threshed and, if desired, milled.

ALENQUER, MY BIRTHPLACE!

But returning to my topic: from the point at which the Tagus bathes Santarém, and continuing down to Lisbon, it follows a very wide and very deep riverbed. Unwilling to be contained by it, the river forms many coves and islands here and there on both of its sides. Along this course one can see fortifications or castles, villages and farmhouses, all laid out with a most agreeable and delightful appearance.

More or less at the midpoint of this stretch of the Tagus, on the western bank, is situated the fortress of Alenquer, which, according to Resende, was called "Gerabriga" in ancient times. It is the land where I was born! Upon delving further into a different interpretation of this name, one arrives at the conclusion that its meaning in the Saxon tongue is "Alanorum ecclesiam." Those of this opinion will not be greatly mistaken.[94]

Indeed, after the Alans slaughtered and burned a devastating path across Europe, they settled in these parts. From what can be gathered from many annals, they lived here until the Goths descended upon them.[95] At that point they were forced to completely quit the province and search out other lands. So ever since the beginning, or almost so, these people have been linked to the Saxons by language, by customs, and by proximity. And even today they feel united through these many bonds of kinship.

At the foot of Alenquer – most of it is situated at the summit of a fairly high hill – a delightful river springs forth from several underground channels of water. Plentiful in fish, it is flanked along both sides by groves of trees whose agreeable shade is enjoyed by a good deal of the inhabitants during the strong, midday heat.

Then, rushing turbulently downhill through a rocky course, it flows on across the plain, emptying into the Tagus some six-thousand paces from its source. At this point the Tagus forms a number of islets, all of which are abundantly endowed with wheat and the richest of pasturelands. However, none of them today can claim the castles, villages or vineyards, of which Strabo has written.[96] Perhaps their absence is due to the flooding of the Tagus, or to the antiquity of that age.

THE TAGUS REIGNS OVER THE WORLD

But such flaws are roundly compensated for through another glorious title: in our day, this same Tagus sets forth the laws and norms on every coast of the Ocean, in Africa and in Asia. The kings and princes of those provinces subject themselves to these laws either freely or by force, rendering service to the Portuguese and ever more frequently bound to the Christian faith. This is marked by the greatest of deference, not only in the realm of the Indies, but also in the territories of the Chinese and the confines of the Japanese, a people unknown in Europe until recently.

In a brief work I published on the fertility and opulence of Hispania, I treated in considerable detail the innumerable exotic things shipped to Lisbon during the course of each year from our possessions in India, Persia, Arabia, Ethiopia, Brazil and Africa. That is why we will purposely make no particular mention of them now. If by chance anyone wishes to acquire a broader understanding, find that book and read it.[97]

CONCLUSION

If, on the other hand, this work of ours does not please the reader, know that I did not do it imagining myself to be the only writer capable of the job. Consequently, should anyone present a more perfect narrative of the origin and circumstances of Lisbon, be aware that such a work will no doubt be well-received by everyone, and gratifying, above all, to me.

THE END

[COLOPHON OF THE FIRST EDITION]

Évora, at the press of André de Burgos, printer to the most illustrious Prince Henrique, Infante of Portugal, Cardinal of the Holy Roman Church, Legate of the Apostolic See. This edition authorized by the Reverend Father Gaspar dos Reis, Doctor of Sacred Theology and Inquisitor of Heretical Depravity. October 1554.

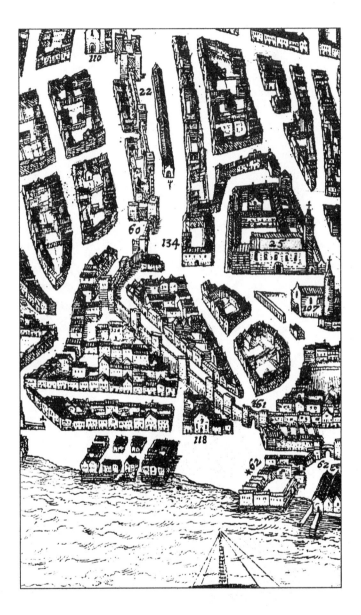

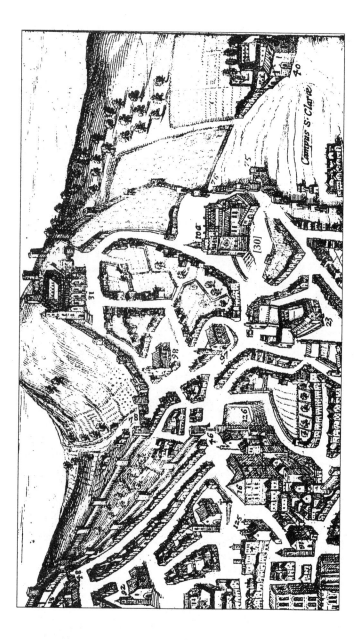

NOTES

1. As a prince not destined to inherit the crown, Henrique bore the Portuguese title *Infante*. During the reign of his brother, João III, he became the titular cardinal of SS. Quattro Coronati, the fourth-century church in Rome. Although João III, like his father Manuel, was a great patron of humanists (such as Góis, Gil Vicente, and André de Resende), Henrique was not. The *Urbis Olisiponis Descriptio* was published in 1554, with João in his final years and Henrique the presumable successor to the throne, as regent of Sebastião. It is likely, therefore, that Góis dedicated this text to him as an act of prudence. Twice already the humanist had been called before the Inquisition, formally established in Portugal in 1536. Only three years after this work's publication, in 1557, Henrique himself would assume still greater power as the Inquisitor General, and surely Góis had been watching this rising star uneasily. Saraiva and Lopes, *História*, 182-83, note that "in 1564 the decisions of the Council of Trent were promulgated in Portugal without restrictions, unlike any other kingdom of Western Europe." For Damião de Góis, this radical change in political and ideological winds meant increased censorship and, ultimately, humiliation and imprisonment as an old man.

2. In fact Góis includes scant references to the Americas – even to Brazil. Portugal was slow to exploit and settle Brazil, focusing instead on the administration of its vast African and Asian commerical routes. Only in 1549 did Portugal send a significant expedition to Brazil. Even thereafter, the French and Dutch would occupy some of its northern and southern coasts for decades.

3. "Dom" is a title of address, equivalent to "Lord." See Appendix B for a chronology of Portuguese monarchs. During the reign of João II (1481 until his death in 1495), much gold and many slaves were imported from Africa, and a new administrative system was established to alleviate the growing pains of a surging empire. These

fiscal and legal reforms were modeled in part on those implanted by João's Spanish contemporaries, Isabel and Ferdinand. The next Portuguese monarch, Manuel I, would benefit greatly from this foundation, extending the far limits of commerce into the East Indies through his agent, Afonso de Albuquerque (1453-1515).

4.   Humanist writers of Góis' time often referred to Africa as Ethiopia; the Greek and Roman authors they emulated normally referred to this continent as Libya.

5.   *Fides, Religio, Moresque Aethiopum...* (Louvain: Rutgero Rescio, 1540). See bibliography for a complete listing of Góis' publications.

6.   This is a reference to the devout Prince Henry the Navigator, who directed the development of Portuguese maritime exploration from his school on the windblown, southwestern cape of Sagres, from 1415 until his death in 1460.

7.   Here Góis refers to the Cape of Good Hope, describing it as the southernmost tip of what seems to be the entire lower lobe of the African continent. His grandiose geographical references direct us through "vast stretches of land" down to a single point. This echoes the Portuguese obsession of the late fifteenth century with sailing south to such a point that would finally carry them on to the riches of India. Góis takes this opportunity to remind his reader that the question of a sea route around Africa was discussed also by his revered ancients. Hence the references here: for Ptolemy (100-178 AD), the waters of the Mountains of the Moon were the source of the Nile, somewhere south of the Equator; flanking the great lobe of lower Africa were the Hesperic Gulf – the sea to the west – and the Prasso Promontory, an unidentified headland jutting out into the Indian Ocean from the coast of present-day Tanzania. Portuguese navigators had supplied the accurate latitude for the Cape, located just north of 35° S. For a brief note on Ptolemy and the many other classical authors invoked by Góis in the *Urbis Olisiponis Descriptio*, see Appendix C.

8.   Góis frequently invokes the writings and opinions of Greeks and Romans, but not blindly. Ptolemy's *Geography* was extremely well-received in Europe during the fifteenth century in its Latin translation, but, as Góis notes here, Portuguese explorations proved that ancient source to be inaccurate. So great was the respect for

Ptolemy during the fifteenth and sixteenth centuries that, even as new and more accurate maps of Africa and the Americas were emerging, the Ptolemaic version featuring an enclosed Indian Ocean (without America, of course) continued to be seen.

9. The "Pillars" refer to the promontories of Gibraltar (Spain) and Jebel Musa (Morocco), at the Strait of Gibraltar. According to the story of Hercules, he planted these formations into the sea while seeking the oxen of Geryon.

10. Hannibal (247-182 BC) was the celebrated leader of the Carthaginians against the Romans in the Second Punic War and, earlier, an agent of Carthaginian expansion in the Iberian Peninsula.

11. Flourished 104-101 BC. A Greek from Ephesus who voyaged along the Spanish Atlantic coast, he wrote eleven geographical books.

12. See Appendix C for brief notes on most of these classical sources.

13. Herodotus states: "For Libya [Africa] is clearly surrounded by the sea except for its boundary with Asia [Sinai]." For him, the Phoenician voyage took over two years. See Herodotus, *The History*, 4.42, trans. David Greene (Chicago: University of Chicago Press, 1987), 295-96.

14. Here Herodotus recounts an aborted attempt to circumnavigate the African continent. The voyage was assigned to Sataspes by Xerxes (Persian king, c.520-465 BC) as punishment for a rape. His task unfulfilled, Sataspes was impaled. Ibid., 4.43 (Greene, 296).

15. See Strabo, *Geography*, 1.2.31, trans. Horace Leonard Jones (Cambridge, MA: Harvard University Press, 1960), 1:139. In Greek mythology, Menelaus was king of Sparta, husband of Helen and brother of Agamemnon. *Gades* refers to Cádiz, Spain. Strabo ultimately seems to discard this voyage as an impossibility.

16. Góis quotes the phrase *"auri sacra fames"* from a passage in the *Aeneid* 3.57: "To what dost thou not drive the hearts of men, O accursed hunger for gold!" See Virgil, *Eclogues, Georgics, Aeneid I-VI*, trans. H. Rushton Fairclough, 2 vols. (Cambridge, MA: Harvard

University Press, 1986), 1:352-53. As scribe for the Portuguese trading center in Antwerp, Góis had become well-acquainted with the economic motives for Portuguese expansion. Here he omits another official apology for empire – the conversion of distant souls to Christianity.

17. A clear exaggeration.

18. For a listing of historical surveys useful for this and other periods covered in the *Urbis Olisiponis Descriptio,* see works by Birmingham, Livermore, Russel-Wood, Serrão, and Wheeler listed in the Bibliography, part C.

19. Claudius Ptolemy, *Geography,* 2.4, roughly confirms Góis' reading as "Oliosipon."

20. See *Geography,* 3.2.13 and 3.4.3.

21. The Turdestani, or Tartessians, were a culturally advanced, non-Celtic people who occupied a region of western Andalucía centered near Cádiz or Huelva. They flourished in the fifth and sixth centuries BC, being influenced then by both Phoenician and Greek traders. Tartessus seems to have collapsed as Celtic tribes moved into that region and gained power. Carthaginian dominion soon followed. Lisbon may have first been established before the Celts, by the Tartessians, who would have built a fortress on or near the site of the later Castle of São Jorge, on the central hill of the city. Evidence for these origins rests in Lisbon's earliest known pre-Roman name, *Olisipo*: the suffix -*ipo* is common to other ancient cities of the Tartessian region in Andalucia. *Olisipo* has also been traced to the Phoenician *allis ubbo,* or "pleasant bay." See p. 50 n. 72 below for the more certain history.

22. Resende (1498-1573) was another prominent Portuguese humanist who, like Góis, lived in Louvain for a time. A number of his works contain references to *"Olisiponem."* For a sampling of Resende's very stylized, humanist poetry, including some correspondence with Góis, see *On Court Life,* ed. and trans. John R.C. Martyn (Bern: Peter Lang, 1990). The volume contains excellent commentary, as well.

23. Pliny the Elder, *Natural History,* 4.117, trans. H. Rackham, 10 vols. (Cambridge, MA: Harvard University Press, 1942). Subdued militarily during the first century BC, Olisipo became important as

the southern terminus of the Roman highway that extended as far north as Bracara Augusta (Braga).

24. By the time Pliny's *Natural History* was written in the first century, the abundant resources of Roman Lusitania – mountains, forests, rivers, minerals, and wildlife – had become famous. In fact, Hispania exported prized racehorses. Pliny characteristically helped convert such fame into legend through the influential exaggerations of his text. In the third century Solinus' *Polyhistor* reworked those legends, including that of the fantastic Lusitanian mares. Note that Góis coyly pits one classical source against another – Justin vs Pliny (et al.) – to conclude only that it would be wise not to pass judgment on the issue. He prefers to admit the legendary as genuine possibility, at least for the sake of embellishing his story, just as he does immediately before on the question of Ulysses. By admitting the conception-by-wind theory he seems to be teasing the reader, winking a friendly eye, as he does elsewhere in the text. Of course, well-crafted, elaborate argument such as this was a classical, and thus humanist, art.

25. Rodrigo Jiménez de Rada (1170-1247) was appointed archbishop of Toledo in 1208 and maintained important connections with the Vatican. His *Historiae de rebus Hispaniae* (1236-43) contains various references to Portugal and Lusitania. Varro is not mentioned, contrary to Góis' assertion here. See the edition prepared by Juan Fernández Valverde (Turnhout: Brepols, 1987).

26. Cabo da Roca is the westernmost point in continental Europe. Its actual distance from Lisbon is twenty miles, making Góis' pace equivalent to a little more than four feet.

27. *Natural History* 9.4 (Rackham 3:169).

28. Medieval travel narratives, such as the *Book of Marco Polo* and the fictional *Travels of Sir John Mandeville*, and cosmographies, such as the *Imago Mundi*, captivated their relatively small readership with fantastic accounts of odd beasts and humans, which routinely appeared on maps, as well. Many of these drew upon the extraordinary tales compiled by Pliny in his *Natural History*, which, like so many classical texts, had been preserved in Greek or Arabic for centuries in Moslem libraries, then reintroduced to European Christendom via twelfth-century Latin translations at Toledo. By

the mid-sixteenth century, however, educated and well-traveled Europeans, such as Damião de Góis, could afford to discriminate more sharply between truth and invention. Here Góis' discourse on the marine-men is calculated to intrigue and entertain his visitors to Lisbon, typically northern Europeans who would sail past this stretch of coastline before entering the Tagus estuary and Lisbon. A good storyteller, he lets the reader draw the conclusion. For more on the medieval and Renaissance travel texts, see Anthony Grafton, *New Worlds, Ancient Texts* (Cambridge, MA: Harvard-Belnap, 1992).

29.   The present-day Oued Sebgag, a salt-flat riverbed that rises in the Djebel Amour Mountains, approximately 150 miles south of Algiers.

30.   Present-day Cabo Espichel is eighteen miles south of the mouth of the Tagus River. To Ptolemy and other writers it was known as *Barbarum* or *Magnum Promontorium*.

31.   Presently an industrial community opposite Lisbon on the south bank of the Tagus estuary.

32.   North Africans crossed the Strait of Gibraltar in 711 and quickly overran the peninsula in the wake of a fragmented Germanic presence. The Christian Reconquest began almost immediately in the north, but lasted centuries. As Góis will narrate, the Portuguese regained their original lands in northern Portugal during the twelfth century. By the late thirteenth century they had also pushed much further south, consolidating most of their modern-day territory. For references to this fundamental period of national formation, see H.V. Livermore, *The Origins of Spain and Portugal* (London: George Allen & Unwin, 1971).

33.   Alfonso VI, of León (1065-1109) and Castile (1072-1109).

34.   Teresa was Alfonso's illegitimate daughter by Jimena Muñoz. With Henrique of Burgundy she had a son, Afonso or Afonso Henriques, who would become Portugal's first king (1140-1185). The Burgundian dynasty, thus established, would last until the end of the reign of Fernando I (1367-1383). It was succeeded by João I of the house of Avis.

35.   Both are cities in south-central Portugal. The events took place in 1139/40.

36. The seventeen-week siege of Lisbon succeeded in October of 1147, thanks not only to the leadership of Afonso Henriques, as Góis dutifully reports, but in great measure to the efforts of foreign crusaders. The Second Crusade's only major success, in fact, was this victory. Composed largely of English, Flemish, and German troops, it stopped in Porto en route to the Holy Land, and then on to Lisbon where a compact was sealed to assist the Portuguese in conquering the Muslim city. This cooperation laid the foundation for the enduring, close ties that followed between England and Portugal. A highly descriptive, eyewitness account was written shortly after the siege – *De expugnatione Lyxbonensi* – and attributed to a chaplain in the service of a major backer within the crusade, Hervey of Glanvill. Since the sixteenth century this chaplain has commonly been called Osbern (based on the ambiguous first line of the text), an attribution still not taken as fact. See *De expugnatione Lyxbonensi: The Conquest of Lisbon,* ed. and trans. Charles Wendell David (New York: Columbia University Press, 1936).

37. Henrique's gravestone is at the church of São Vicente de Fora, founded in the year of his death, which occurred at the siege of Lisbon. He is also known as the Knight of the Palm, since legend had it that a palm grew over his grave, endowed with curative powers. Hence the miracles mentioned here by Góis. From this legend also comes the name of the Rua da Palma.

38. This cathedral of Lisbon was begun shortly after the successful siege of the city in 1147, built on the site of the main mosque of the Moslem city. The façade shows the plain, Romanesque style; the chapels and cloister are Gothic; and the choir, baroque. The Sé suffered considerable damage during the earthquake of 1755 and was later restored. Saint Vincent was martyred in 304 at Valencia; his remains were transferred to Lisbon's Sé Cathedral in 1173.

39. André de Resende's poem on the saint, "Vincentius levita et martyr," was originally published in Lisbon by Luis Rodrigues in 1545. For a modern edition, see *Vincentius levita et martyr,* ed. José V. de Pina Martins (Paris: Touzot, 1981).

40. At this battle Castilian and Portuguese armies frustrated the last Moorish attempt at reconquering the peninsula.

41. Saint Anthony was born at this site in 1195 and later gained fame for his works in Padua. As patron saint of Lisbon, his feast day of June 13 is celebrated each year with great revelry.

42. The meaning of this word is unclear. Felicidade Alves, *Descrição da Cidade de Lisboa,* 42, notes that Raul Machado offers the interpretation "above the choir loft of the chapel...."

43. Roman Lisbon stretched down the western flank of the central hill, but Góis seems to be referring to the Moorish, Jewish, and Christian occupation of the Alfama zone, more to the east. His estimation of the estuary's widest point is quite close to the actual distance of about five miles.

44. Aldeia Galega today is subsumed within the city of Montijo. Coina still exists.

45. The Arabic place name *Almada*, for a large city near the point of this coastline, was apparently understood to mean "mines of gold and silver." Its literal meaning is "point." It is about 1.7 miles from Lisbon, about half the distance offered by Góis.

46. Adiça is a beach-front area a few miles north of Cabo Espichel. In *Natural History* 4.115 Pliny writes "the Tagus is famous for its auriferous sands." Of Portugal's rivers, Strabo asserts that "most of them...contain very great quantities of gold-dust...." *Geography,* 3.3.4.

47. A pre-Roman, Celtic people who inhabited not so much the southern or even central parts of Portugal, as suggested here by Góis, but rather the northern area between the Mondego and Douro rivers.

48. Cascais was a well-fortified town in Góis' time, a naturally strategic point along the Atlantic coastline. The first edition of Georg Braun, *Civitates orbis terrarum,* vol. 1 (Cologne: Georg Braun, 1593), featured a smaller print of "Cascale" alongside the main print showing Lisbon. Today Cascais is a small, wealthy city connected to Lisbon via the seaside highway and train line.

49. Near present-day Oeiras.

50. Today Belém – "Bethlehem" – is a district within the bounds of Lisbon. A major cultural and tourist center was built there along the shore in 1992 to commemorate the fifth centenary of Columbus' first voyage, and the subsequent age of Atlantic voyages by

both Spaniards and Portuguese. In this section of the text Góis describes Belém's major attractions.

51. In 1459 Prince Henry had a small chapel built for sailors departing on voyages to Africa and the Atlantic islands. On that site Manuel began construction for his ambitious cathedral and monastery in the year 1496, with planning beginning only in 1502, when profits from the recently-arrived Indian pepper shipments permitted such expenses. Only in 1551 was construction completed, allowing for the burial there of the late King Manuel, Vasco da Gama, and, in 1580, the poet of the epic *Os Lusíadas*, Luis de Camões. The architects Diogo de Boytaca and João de Castilho used this major project to articulate the late-Gothic style that came to be known as Manueline. Its carved-stone motifs include twisted ropes, anchors, nets, shells, flowers, leaves, fruit, and the ever-present armillary sphere that Manuel took for a symbol of empire. The Jerónimos is generally considered the last Gothic cathedral of Europe, although some Portuguese historians consider it to be a separate style in itself.

52. "King Dom Manuel, greatest of all monarchs, erected on the shore / a vast and splendid temple, dedicated to the mother of God. / His heir, in dominion and piety, enlarged the work; / equals in faith, both vie for pre-eminence in their structure."

53. The Tower of Belém was conceived as a massive, yet compact, fortress for the defense of the city, further up river. It was built between 1515 and 1521. A view of the tower from the Tagus can be found in the book published by its engraver, Pieter van den Berghe, *Theatrum Hispaniae* (Amsterdam: n.p, 1695).

54. This estimate results in a distance of about 2.5 miles, instead of the actual four miles' distance between Belém and the outer edge of sixteenth-century Lisbon. The western wall of the city passed just inside the Rua do Alecrim, running down toward the present-day Cais do Sodré train station.

55. Today's traveler from Belém toward the old city center of Lisbon finds few such sights. The much-expanded shipping industry now hugs a long stretch of this shoreline. The shipyards and docks of Góis' time were clustered around the Ribeira das Naus, the Terreiro do Paço, and the old Ribeira, fronting the heart of the city.

56. Góis will end this tour with a stop at the Convent of Santa Clara, which he calls the "northernmost" point of Lisbon. The progression is more realistically from west to east, rather than from south to north.

57. These Christians were martyred in 304 AD at the time of Emperor Diocletian and the governor Dacian. Their holy day is celebrated October 1.

58. Originally a Manueline chapel. João III gave the land on which it stood to the Jesuits, who converted it to a highly decorated church in the mannerist style, late in the century. This work was directed by the Italian architect Filippo Terzi, whose influence upon Lisbon's building around 1600 was extreme. The Church of São Roque features elaborate tile panels painted by Francisco de Matos in 1584.

59. This descent is near the present-day Escadinhas do Duque, crossing just north of the Rossio in what is now Restauradores. The Restauradores Plaza was largely a nineteenth-century innovation (though begun in 1764) and known then as the Passeio Público.

60. The Anunciada Church and its cloister were completed during the first half of the sixteenth century. In 1542 it was donated to the Jesuits, who established a school there, lending the structure its familiar name of Coleginho.

61. The Mouraria extends down the back side of the Castle of São Jorge, to the north, and was a district falling outside the city walls. For the Moors who chose to remain after the siege of Lisbon in 1147, religious practice was, of course, extremely limited. Góis refers to the Moors by the term "Saracens," originally a Greek name for the nomadic Arab peoples of the Middle East. On the southeastern side of the castle and within the city walls lived most of Lisbon's Jews. This district was known as the *Alfama*, or, in reference to a more restricted zone closer to the bank of the Tagus, the *Judiaria*. Hoping to gain the hand of Isabel of Spain (daughter of Ferdinand and Isabel), King Manuel issued a proclamation in 1496 that forced both Muslims and Jews to convert or leave the country. Many of the Jews had only recently arrived from Spain, following the expulsion there in 1492. In the late 1490s, then, there was an exodus of skilled administrators and professionals from Portugal. Most of the Jews in this group settled in Antwerp and other northern

European cities, where they came to serve as a marketing arm of the Portuguese empire as it expanded in the sixteenth century. Naturally, in Portugal their absence was deeply felt within the administrative tiers. In 1506, with the plague ravaging the city, mobs massacred Jews, razing their property, and converting synagogues into churches.

62. The Igreja dos Anjos is not found on the Braun map, as it would lie directly behind the castle. Góis is describing here the north-south valley between Anjos and the Igreja da Nossa Senhora do Monte (to the right, or east). This valley may be considered the right-hand arm of a low-lying area of the city, shaped like a "Y". Today the Rua da Palma and the Avenida Almirante Reis run through it. The left-hand arm includes Restauradores and the modern Avenida da Liberdade. The two branches meet around the Praça da Figueira (just east of Rossio), then run south through the Baixa to the shore of the Tagus. This "Y" was actually an inlet of the Tagus estuary during Roman times. The water had receded by the late thirteenth century.

63. The monastery and church were built within the city walls in 1271, expanded in stages during the sixteenth century with both Manueline and mannerist details, then partially reconstructed after suffering damage in the earthquake. The church contains some very personalized and even whimsical tile paintings. A sweeping, panoramic view of the city can be had from Graça.

64. This church was founded outside ("fora") the early city walls in 1147 by Afonso Henriques as thanksgiving for his victory at Lisbon against the Moors. Its Romanesque and Gothic details were built over in the mannerist style between 1582 and 1629 at the behest of Philip II. The Italian architect Filippo Terzi conceived the design.

65. Here Góis' measurement is a bit high, compared to the actual distance of about 1.5 miles.

66. Seven, not five, hills were cited in the 17th century by Nicolau de Oliveira, *Livro das grandezas de Lisboa* (Lisbon: Impressão Régia, 1804), to liken the city to Rome and its ancient splendors.

67. This estimated distance around the perimeter – a little over five miles – was a bit high. Actual distance was closer to four miles. Góis wisely qualifies his measurements of the city by referring to its precipitous terrain.

68. If each household were comprised of four people, the population of the city would then be 80,000. Other estimates are roughly in agreement. In 1527 a royal census counted about 60,000, while Rodriques de Oliveira's *Sumário* of 1551 reports 90,997 persons in Lisbon. See "A população de Lisboa," *Olisipo* 2 (1939): 13-83.

69. Sarmatia was an ancient region of Slavic nomads north of the Black Sea, formerly home to the Alan tribes, and sometimes used (incorrectly) to refer to Poland. Damião de Góis may have journeyed through part of Sarmatia en route to Vilnius, Lithuania.

70. The double streams of this fountain, the Chafariz Novo, may correspond to the one seen clearly near the water's edge in Braun's map.

71. As noted in the introduction, this section of the text constitutes one of the author's most outrageous exaggerations. Curiously, João Brandão's 1552 accounting of the situation of the city also exalts the water supply. See *Grandeza e Abastança de Lisboa em 1552,* ed. José da Felicidade Alves (Lisbon: Livros Horizonte, 1990), 103-6. In reality, few fountains existed, their waters were of poor quality, and occasional droughts would cause the populace to take to the streets in processions, begging the heavens for water. See Fernando Castelo-Branco, *Lisboa Seiscentista* (Lisbon: Câmara Municipal, 1956), 375-76. The sixteenth-century Portuguese painter Francisco de Holanda (1517-1584) confirms this in his *Da fábrica que falece na cidade de Lisboa,* ed. Joaquim Vasconcelos (Porto: Imprensa Portuguesa, 1875). There exists today in the Baixa section of the city (at the Rua da Prata and Rua da Conceição) the underground remains of a vast Roman bath or reservoir. It is open to visits only a few days a year, due to frequent flooding.

72. Since earliest times the city existed as a fortified town upon this central hill. The original Celtic *castro* – one of thousands that dotted Portugal's hills during the early first milennium BC– grew during Roman times but became more important during the Moorish period. The walls of the Moorish castle were defended with ten towers, and extended down past Santa Luzia to the Chafariz d'El Rei (on the east) and by the Church of St. Anthony of Padua to the Misericórdia (on the west). Inside the castle was the palace of the Alcáçova, which was later inhabited by Portuguese monarchs from Dinis (reigned 1279-1325) to Manuel. By the fourteenth century it had come to be called the Castle of Saint George.

It was Manuel who moved the royal residence to the shore (to his new Paço da Ribeira), in order to be closer to the intense new commerce along the port. King Sebastian (reigned 1557-1578) chose to live in the Alcáçova. Most of the palace, but not the castle, was destroyed in the earthquake. Today the castle offers perhaps the most spectacular view of the city and Tagus estuary, and features small gardens and fountains, peacocks, swans, and other wildlife.

73. Here Góis follows his humanist instincts, choosing the number seven for its special connotations (the seven days of the week as described in Genesis 1:1-2:3, Rome's seven hills, etc.). Góis may have intended his visitors to tour one building per day during a week-long visit.

74. *Misericórdia* = compassion, mercy. The southern façade – doorway and windows – were left standing after the earthquake and were incorporated into the reconstruction there that became the new home of the Igreja da Conceição. The Misericórdia itself then occupied one of the buildings at nearby São Roque.

75. This hospital, begun in 1492 and completed by Manuel, formed the eastern flank of the Rossio Plaza. An excellent view of its Gothic façade, prominent steps, and arcades is found in a print published in 1757. The hospital and Rossio are also the subject of an eighteenth-century tile panel, found today at the Museu da Cidade. Todos-os-Santos disappeared with the earthquake, but a few columns, capitals, and moldings have been preserved.

76. The Rossio was, along with the Ribeira Market, one of the city's most popular public spaces. It was defined with the enlargement of the city walls by Fernando in 1373 and came to be the venue of bullfights and autos-da-fe (the processions and executions of the Inquisition). Its sixteenth-century borders included the Todos-os-Santos Hospital (east), the Paço dos Estaus and offices of the Inquisition (north) and, rising in the west, the Convento and Igreja of Carmo. During the post-quake reconstruction of Lisbon the Rossio space was largely retained, with its layout straightened a bit.

77. Or, more accurately, the "Y" described above, p. 49 n. 62.

78. The Estaus Palace dates to 1450 and actually lay to the north of the Rossio, not west. It later housed the Inquisition, and, when leveled in 1755, was replaced with the present neoclassical Teatro Nacional de Dona Maria II.

79. This is apparently a criticism of extravagant royal spending.

80. The Carmo was erected in 1389 upon orders of Nuno Álvares Pereira in fulfillment of a vow made at the battle of Aljubarrota. The earthquake destroyed the roof but left standing the Gothic arches and apse, still highly visible from the Baixa below. The interior walls boast several elaborate, blue-and-white tile panels in the style typical of the eighteenth century. The apse, still covered, houses a small museum of astonishing diversity, covering all periods of Portuguese history, and more.

81. A sixteenth-century view of this busy street is seen on a page of the prayer book *Livro de horas de Dom Manuel*, presently at the Museu Nacional de Arte Antiga, Lisbon. Reference to the diversity of the street's shopkeepers (sixteen kinds in all) is made in João Brandão's *Grandeza e Abastança de Lisboa em 1552:* "It seems very disorderly for such a noble street to have such a mixture. Your Highness should order it changed, for the greater nobility of the land, city, and the kingdom" (Felicidade Alves ed., 100).

82. On the general impact of print and the extent of literacy during this period see Elizabeth L. Eisenstein, *The Printing Press as an Agent of Change,* 2 vols. (Cambridge: Cambridge University Press, 1979); Lucien Febvre and Henri-Jean Martin, *The Coming of the Book: The Impact of Printing 1450-1800* (London & New York: Verso, 1990), 287-319; and Tessa Watt, *Cheap Print and Popular Piety, 1550-1640* (Cambridge & New York: Cambridge University Press, 1994).

83. Gois is correct. The commercial hub of the city was found along both sides of the Rua Nova dos Mercadores, especially the several blocks above its northern side. The southern side, of course, gave way to the bustling Terreiro do Paço, a wide space flanked by the Royal Palace along the western edge and, to the east, the Customs Office and Public Granary. This larger district was certainly the busiest, wealthiest, and most densely populated in the city, making it the neighborhood of choice for highlighting to a visitor the "grandeur" of Lisbon.

84. Góis takes the true east for north in his discussion. Moving east, the Rua Nova dos Mercadores approaches the Misericórdia, which then opens onto the wide marketplace of the Praça da Ribeira. Note that Braun's map depicts many small fishing vessels

moored here. This stretch of shoreline fronts the part of Moorish Lisbon established before the 1147 siege by Afonso Henriques. Its eastern- and westernmost points – approximately the Chafariz d'El Rei and the Misericórdia – stood where the old Moorish walls came down to the Tagus from the castle, enclosing the heart of the pre-Portuguese city. Today's tourist will find the Casa dos Bicos in this area, on the Rua dos Bacalhoeiros (Codsellers Street). Its eccentric, diamond-pointed rustication was built into the façade when Brás de Albuquerque – son of the governor of India – erected the house in 1522.

85.   João Brandão also provides a wealth of colorful detail about the Ribeira Market. The Museu da Cidade houses a tile panel depicting the fishmongers at work at the Ribeira, with the Casa dos Bicos at rear.

86.   Here Góis criticizes the government, though he quickly backs away.

87.   Ceuta and Melilla are small Spanish enclaves on the Mediterranean coast of Morocco. Góis probably uses the term "war" to refer to the Christian struggle against Islam, very much alive as a motivator in the Portuguese expansion of the fifteenth and sixteenth centuries.

88.   This tower was beautified considerably in a radical alteration designed by the Italian Filippo Terzi, around 1600. The Braun map shows the older building; for excellent views of the newer one and nearby sites, see van den Berghe, *Theatrum Hispaniae*, pls. 55-62.

89.   The Arsenal was destroyed by the earthquake. Its site is now occupied by the Praça do Município and the Câmara Municipal (Town Hall), begun in 1866.

90.   Damião de Góis traveled extensively through Europe but never set foot in Africa or Asia.

91.   For an evocative description of a Holy Thursday procession, see João Brandão, 121-22. As for the musical compositions of Góis that have survived to our time, all are for voices. One of these, "Nec laetaris," was recorded at the monastery of São Vicente de Fora by the Conservatório Nacional de Lisboa Madrigalistas. See Voz do Dono label, 1976, #8E 065-40 427.

92. A good reference on thirteenth- to nineteenth-century Portuguese *solares*, or villas, is Carlos de Azevedo, *Solares Portuguesas* (Lisbon: Livros Horizonte, 1969).

93. *Natural History*, 4.22 (Rackham, 2:211). The name means "Garrison of Julius."

94. The Celtic suffix *-briga* referred to a small town or fortified camp, equivalent to the later, Latin terms *oppidum* and *castrum* as applied by the Romans. Regarding the origin of Alenquer's modern name, Hirsch, 193, casts doubt on Góis' scholarship of the Saxon language, leaving unresolved the meaning of *Alenquer*.

95. The first Visigothic invasion took place in 419, effectively evicting the Alans from Lusitania.

96. Describing the island opposite Almeirim, near this site, Strabo writes that it is endowed with "fine groves and vines." *Geography* 3.3.1.

97. *Hispania* (Louvain: Rutgero Rescio, 1541 and 1542). This text was written as a rebuttal to the description of Iberia published by Sebastian Münster (1489-1552) in his 1541 publication *Cosmographei*, and deemed unjust by Góis. On folio 19v he mentions Cortés and Pizarro, a rare reference to the Americas for Góis (as is the one to Brazil here).

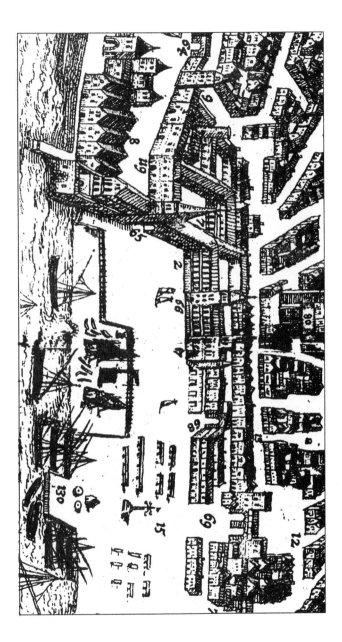

APPENDIX A
A BRIEF CHRONOLOGY OF PORTUGAL
FROM THE 13TH CENTURY

1256	Lisbon becomes the capital of Portugal
1291	Augustine convent begun at Graça
1373-75	King Fernando builds expanded city walls
1383	Crisis and consolidation of monarchy
1389	Convento do Carmo begun
1420	Prince Henrique establishes navigational center at Sagres, initiating African voyages
1487	Bartolomeo Dias sails to Cape of Good Hope
1492	Hospital de Todos-os-Santos begun
1495	Manuel I assumes throne
1496-98	Royal edict demands conversion or departure of Jews, accompanied by confiscation of property and destruction of synagogues
1497	Vasco da Gama sails to India
1499	Convento dos Jerónimos (Belém) begun
1500	Construction begins on new royal residence, the Paço da Ribeira, by the port; Pedro Álvares Cabral lands at Brazil
1506	Massacre of Jews provoked by Dominicans in Lisbon
1513	Bairro Alto neighborhood first laid out
1515	Torre de Belém begun
1521	João III assumes throne
1523	Casa dos Bicos begun
1531	Earthquake
1534	Igreja da Misericórdia begun
1536	Inquisition established in Portugal
1555	Igreja de São Roque begun
1556	Igreja da Graça begun
1557	Sebastião assumes throne
1578	King Sebastião's army vanquished at Alcácer Quibir, in North Africa

1578	Cardinal Henrique assumes throne
1580	Spain's King Phillip II absorbs Portugal into his kingdom. Italian architect Filippo Terzi begins alterations at Igreja de São Vicente de Fora
1581	Terzi begins alterations at Paço da Ribeira

APPENDIX B
MONARCHS OF PORTUGAL, 1140-1598

Afonso Henriques (Afonso I), 1140-85
Sancho I, 1185-1211
Afonso II, 1211-23
Sancho II, 1223-46
Afonso III, 1246-79
Dinis, 1279-1325
Afonso IV, 1325-57
Pedro I, 1357-67
Fernando I, 1367-83
João I, 1384-1433
Duarte I, 1433-38
Afonso V, 1438-81
João II, 1481-95
Manuel I, 1495-1521
João III, 1521-57
Sebastião I, 1557-78
Cardinal Henrique, 1578-80
Phillip I (Phillip II of Spain), 1580-98

APPENDIX C
CLASSICAL AUTHORS REFERRED TO IN THE URBIS OLISIPONIS DESCRIPTIO

Aristonarcus (1st c. BC) Alexandrian grammarian of the Augustan age who wrote commentaries on Hesiod and Pindar.
Eudoxus (c.400-c.350 BC) Leading mathematician and astronomer of the generation before Euclid.

APPENDICES

Herodotus (484?-425 BC) Early Greek historian; author of *The Histories.* Known as the "Father of History."

Juba II (c.46 BC-c.23 AD) Numidian, raised in Italy. Attempted to inculcate Greek and Roman culture in his vast domains in North Africa.

Justinus, Marcus Junianus (fl. c. 250 AD) Also known as Justin. Wrote epitome of Pompeius Trogus' *Historiae Philippicae,* influential text in the Middle Ages.

Martianus Cabella (410-439 AD) Latin author from Carthage whose nine-book prose and poetry work, *De nuptiis Mercurii et Philologiae,* collected a great variety of information.

Mela, Pomponius (fl. c.43 AD) Born near Gibraltar. Author of early Latin geography, *De situ orbis.*

Nepos, Cornelius (c.100-c.25 BC) Roman biographer and historian.

Pliny the Elder (23/24-79 AD) Roman writer of the massive *Natural History,* a famous compendium of both true and outrageous assertions culled from history and natural sciences. Born in northern Italy, educated in Rome.

Ptolemaeus, Claudius (c.100-c.178 AD) Greek geographer, mathematician, and astronomer, born in Upper Egypt, worked in Alexandria. His *Geography* lists 8,000 places, each with a latitude and longitude, and includes a final book of maps that exerted great influence in the Arabic and Christian worlds until c.1500.

Solinus, Julius (fl. after 200 AD) Latin author whose *Polyhistor* was based very much on the *Natural History* of Pliny and *De situ orbis* of Pomponius Mela.

Strabo (64 BC-24 AD) Greek geographer from Pontus who traveled the greater eastern Mediterranean region and wrote *Geography,* an ambitious and colorful attempt to locate the peoples of the world on a single continent with a grid system and describe their varied customs. This book was influential through the Middle Ages, and generally more reliable than Pliny's *Natural History.*

Varro, Marcus Terentius (116-27 BC) Latin writer, librarian, and praetor who fought in Spain and is known for only two of many books written: *De lingua latina* and *Rerum rusticarum libri III.*

Xenophon (c.428-c.350 BC) Athenian writer on a great variety of topics.

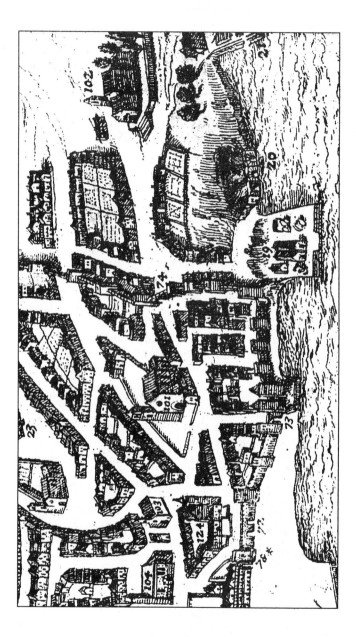

BIBLIOGRAPHY

A. WORKS BY GÓIS

LATIN WRITINGS

As Cartas Latinas de Damião de Góis. Ed. Amadeu Torres. Paris: Fundação Calouste Gulbenkian, Centro Cultural Português, 1982.

Comentarii rerum gestarum in India 1538 citra Gangem. Louvain: Rutgero Rescio, 1539. An Italian version appeared in Venice, 1539, and a German version in Augsburg, 1540.

De bello cambaico ultimo commentarii tres. Louvain: Servatius Zassenus de Diest, 1549.

Deploratio Lappianae Gentis. Louvain: Rutgero Rescio, 1540, 1541, 1544. Originally appended to the 1532 edition of *Legatio Magni Indorum....*

De rebus et imperio Lusitanorum ad Paulum Jovium disceptatiuncula. Louvain: Rutgero Rescio, 1539.

Fides, Religio, Moresque Aethiopum sub Imperio Preciosi Joannis degentium Damiano a Goes ac Paulo Jovio interpretibus. Louvain: Rutgero Rescio, 1540; Paris: Christian Wechelum, 1541; Louvain: Rutgero Rescio, 1544.

—. as "The Deploration of the Peoples of Lappia" and "The Faith, Religion and Manners of the Aethiopians." In *The Manners, Lawes and Customes of All Nations.* Ed. and trans. E. Aston, London: George Eld, 1611.

Hispania or *Hispaniae Urbis Ubertia et Potentia.* Louvain: Rutgero Rescio, 1541, 1542, 1544.

Lappiae Descriptio. Louvain: Rutgero Rescio, 1542.

Legatio Magni Indorum Imperatoris Presbyteri Joannis ad Emanuelem Lusitaniae Regem in 1513. Antwerp: Johannes Grapheus, 1532.

—. Republished with some changes. Antwerp: Martin Nutius, 1544. English and German versions appeared in 1533. A Dutch edition was published in 1616.

61

Noese e crise na epistolografia latina goisiana. Ed. and trans. Amadeu Torres. Paris: Fundação Calouste Gulbenkian, Centro Cultural Português, 1982.

Oratio Postliminio ad Universitatem. Louvain: Rutgero Rescio, 1543.

Urbis Lovaniensis Obsidio. Lisbon: Luis Rodrigues, 1546.

Urbis Olisiponis Descriptio. Évora: André de Burgos, 1554. Subsequent Latin editions were published in 1602, 1603 and 1791.

Portuguese Writings

"As Cartas Portuguesas de Damião de Góis e Memoriais Escritos na Prisão." In Aubrey Bell, *Damião de Góis, A Portuguese Humanist.* Trans. and ed. António Álvaro Dória as *Um Humanista Português. Cultura Literária: Estudios Diversos.* Ser. A. Lisbon: n.p., 1942.

Chronica do Felicissimo Rei Dom Emanuel. Lisbon: Francisco Corrêa, 1566-67.

Chronica do Principe Dom Joam, Rey que foi destes reynos segundo do nome. Lisbon: Francisco Corrêa, 1567.

Descrição da Cidade de Lisboa. Trans. and ed. José da Felicidade Alves. Lisbon: Livros Horizonte, 1988.

Lisboa de Quinhentos: Descrição de Lisboa. Trans. Raúl Machado. Lisbon: Livraria Avelar Machado, 1937.

Livro de Marco Tullio Ciceram, chamado Catam maior. Venice: Stevam Sabio, 1538.

Nobiliário de Portugal. This unfinished manuscript was lost some time after 1622, according to José da Felicidade Alves (*Descrição da Cidade de Lisboa,* 15). Copies exist in the National Libraries in Lisbon and Madrid.

Musical Compositions

"*Nec laeteris inimica mea....*" In *Dodecachordon.* Basel: Henricus Glareanus, 1547. This motet for three voices has been recorded by the Conservatório Nacional de Lisboa Madrigalistas, published by Voz do Dono, #8E 065-40 427, Lisbon: 1976.

"*Surge, propera amica mea.*" In *Cantiones septem, sex et quinque vocum: Longe gravissimae, iuxta ac amoenissimae, in Germania maxime hactenus typis non excusae.* Augsburg: Sigismund Salminger, 1545.

B. OTHER PRIMARY SOURCES

Berghe, Pieter van den. *Theatrum Hispaniae*. Amsterdam: Berghe, n.d. [c.1695].

Brandão, João. *Grandeza e Abastança de Lisboa em 1552*. Ed. José da Felicidade Alves. Lisbon: Livros Horizonte, 1990.

Braun, Georg, and Frans Hogenberg. *Civitates orbis terrarum*. Vol. 5. Cologne: Georg Braun, 1598.

Bruni, Leonardo. *The Humanism of Leonardo Bruni: Selected Texts*. Ed. and trans. Gordon Griffiths, James Hankins, David Thompson. Binghamton, NY: Medieval and Renaissance Texts and Studies and Renaissance Society of America, 1987.

Conquista de Lisboa aos Mouros em 1147: Carta de um cruzado Inglês. Ed. José da Felicidade Alves. Lisbon: Livros Horizonte, 1989.

Chaplain Osbern (attrib.). *De expugnatione Lyxbonensi: The Conquest of Lisbon*. Ed. and trans. Charles Wendell David. New York: Columbia University Press, 1936.

Descriptio Urbis: The Roman Census of 1527. Ed. Egmont Lee. Rome: Bulzoni Editore, 1985.

Epistolae Sadoleti, Bembi, et aliorum clarissimorum virorum ad Damianum a Goes equitem Lusitanum. Louvain: Rutgero Rescio, 1543.

Herodotus. *The History*. Trans. David Greene. Chicago: University of Chicago Press, 1987.

Holanda, Francisco de. *Da Fábrica que falece à cidade de Lisboa*. Ed. Joaquim Vasconcelos. Porto: Imprensa Portuguesa, 1875.

Jiménez de Rada, Rodrigo. *Historia de rebus Hispaniae*. Ed. Juan Fernández Valverde. Turnhout: Brepols, 1987.

López, Tomás. *Mapa General del Reyno de Portugal*. Madrid: n.p., 1778.

Nunes Tinoco, João. *Map of Lisbon*. Lisbon: n.p., 1650.

Oliveira, Nicolau de. *Livro das grandezas de Lisboa*. Lisbon: Impressão Régia, 1804.

Pliny the Elder. *Natural History*. Trans. H. Rackham. Cambridge, MA: Harvard University Press, 1942.

Ptolemy, Claudius. *Geography*. Trans. Edward Luther Stevenson; ed. Joseph Fischer, SJ. New York: New York Public Library, 1932.

Rêgo, Raul, ed. *O processo de Damião de Góis na Inquisição*. Lisbon: Edições Excelsior, 1971.

Resende, André de. *Obras portuguesas de André de Resende*. Ed. José Pereira Tavares. Lisbon: Sá da Costa, n.d.

—. *On Court Life*. Ed. and trans. John R.C. Martyn. Bern: Peter Lang, 1990.

—. *Vincentius levita et martyr*. Ed. José V. de Pina Martins. Paris: Touzot, 1981.

Rodrigues de Oliveira, Cristóvão. *Lisboa em 1551: Sumário*. Ed. José da Felicidade Alves. Lisbon: Livros Horizonte, 1987.

Strabo. *Geography*. Ed. E.H. Warmington. Tran. Horace Leonard Jones. 8 vols. London: W. Heinemann, 1917.

Vicente, Gil. *Four Plays of Gil Vicente*. Ed. and trans. Aubrey Bell. Cambridge: Cambridge University Press, 1920. Rprnt. New York: Kraus Reprint, 1969.

Wyngaerde, Anton van den. *Spanish Cities of the Golden Age: The Views of Anton van den Wyngaerde*. Ed. Richard L. Kagan. Los Angeles: University of California Press, 1989.

C. SECONDARY WORKS

Adams, Robert P. *The Better Part of Valor: More, Erasmus, Colet and Vives on Humanism, War and Peace 1496-1535*. Seattle: University of Washington Press, 1962.

Alcalá, Ángel. *El proceso inquisitorial de Fray Luis de León*. Salamanca: Junta de Castilla y León, 1991.

Almeida, João de, et al. *Lisboa das Descobertas*. Lisbon: DistriCultural, 1983.

Anderson, James M., and M. Sheridan Lea. *Portugal: 1001 Sights. An Archaeological and Historical Guide*. Calgary: University of Calgary Press; London: Robert Hale, 1994.

Anselmo, A.J. *Bibliografia das Obras Impressas em Portugal no Século XVI*. Lisbon: Biblioteca Nacional, 1926.

"A população de Lisboa." *Olisipo* 2 (1939): 13-83.

Asênsio, Eugênio. "El italiano Britonio, cantor de la Lisboa de D. João III." *Arquivos do Centro Cultural Português* 5 (1972): 546-59.

"As sete colinas de Lisboa." *Olisipo* 8.29 (Jan. 1945): 179-91.

Atlas de Lisboa: A Cidade no Espaço e no Tempo. Ed. João Soares. Lisbon: Contexto, 1993.

Azevedo, Carlos de. *Solares portugueses*. Lisbon: Livros Horizonte, 1969.

—. and Chester E.V. Brummel. *Churches of Portugal*. New York: Scala Books, 1985.

Bataillon, Marcel, J.-C. Margolin, et al. *Damião de Góis, Humaniste Européen*. Ed. José V. de Pina Martins. Paris: Touzot, 1982.

BIBLIOGRAPHY

Batllori, Miguel. *Humanismo y Renacimiento: Estudios hispano-europeos.* Barcelona: Ariel, 1987.

Birmingham, David. *A Concise History of Portugal.* Cambridge: Cambridge University Press, 1993.

Boyajian, James C. *Portuguese Trade in Asia under the Hapsburgs, 1580-1640.* Baltimore: Johns Hopkins University Press, 1993.

Brearley, Mary. *Hugo Gurgeny: Prisoner of the Lisbon Inquisition.* New Haven: Yale University Press, 1948.

Brown, Jonathan, and Richard G. Mann. *Spanish Painting of the Fifteenth through Nineteenth Centuries.* Washington, DC: National Gallery of Art, 1990.

Caamaño, Jesús María, ed. *Relaciones Artísticas entre Portugal y España.* Salamanca: Junta de Castilla y León, Consejería de Educación y Cultura, 1986.

Caio Velloso, Júlio. *Catálogo das Obras Impressas nos séculos XV e XVI.* Lisbon: Santa Casa da Misericórdia de Lisboa, 1992.

Castelo-Branco, Fernando. *Breve História da Olisipografia.* Amadora: Instituto de Cultura Portuguesa, 1980.

—. *Lisboa seiscentista.* Lisbon: Câmara Municipal, 1956.

Clair, Colin. *A History of European Printing.* London: Academic Press, 1976.

Cornell, Tim, and John Matthews. *Atlas of the Roman World.* New York: Facts on File, 1982.

Cortesão, Armando. *Cartografia e cartógrafos portugueses dos séculos XV e XVI.* 2 vols. Lisbon: Seará Nova, 1935.

Dias, Pedro. "A Viagem de D. Manuel a Espanha e o Surto Mudejar na Arquitectura Portuguesa." In Caamaño, *Relaciones*, 111-28.

Di Camillo, Ottavio. "Humanism in Spain." In *Renaissance Humanism.* Ed. Albert Rabil, Jr. 3 vols. Philadelphia: University of Pennsylvania Press, 1988, 2:55-108.

Eisenstein, Elizabeth L. *The Printing Press as an Agent of Change.* 2 vols. Cambridge: Cambridge University Press, 1979.

Faria, Francisco Leite de. *Estudos bibliográficos sobre Damião de Góis e a sua Época.* Lisbon: Secretária de Estado da Cultura, 1977.

Fasoli, Gina. "La coscienza civica nelle 'Laudes civitatum'." In *La coscienza cittadina nei comuni italiani del Duecento. Atti dell' XI Convegno del Centro di studi sulla spiritualità medievale.* Ed. Giuseppe Ermini. Todi: Accademia Tudertina, 1972, 9-44.

Febvre, Lucien, and Henri-Jean Martin. *The Coming of the Book: The Impact of Printing, 1450-1800.* Trans. David Gerard. London & New York: Verso, 1990.

França, José-Augusto. *Lisboa pombalina e o iluminismo.* Lisbon: Livros Horizonte, 1965.

—. *Lisboa: Urbanismo e Arquitectura.* Amadora: Instituto de Cultura e Lingua Portuguesa, 1980.

Frugoni, Chiara. *A Distant City: Images of Urban Experience in the Medieval World.* Trans. William McCuaig. Princeton: Princeton University Press, 1991.

Gaspar, Jorge. "Aspectos da dinâmica funcional do centro de Lisboa." In *Estudos de geografia urbana* 3. Lisbon: Centro de Estudos Geográficos, Instituto de Alta Cultura, 1972, 9-11.

Goulão, Maria-José. "Alguns Problemas Ligados ao Emprego de Azulejos 'mudéjares' em Portugal nos Séculos XV e XVI." In Caamaño, *Relaciones*, 129-54.

Grafton, Anthony. *New Worlds, Ancient Texts.* Cambridge, MA: Harvard-Belnap, 1992.

Harvey, P.D.A. "Local and Regional Cartography in Medieval Europe." In *The History of Cartography.* Vol. 1. Ed. J.B. Harley and David Woodward. Chicago: University of Chicago Press, 1987.

Hirsch, Elizabeth Feist. *Damião de Góis: The Life and Thought of a Portuguese Humanist.* The Hague: Martinus Nijhoff, 1967.

Hohenberg, Paul M., and Lynn Hollen Lees. *The Making of Urban Europe, 1000-1950.* Cambridge: Harvard University Press, 1985.

Hyde, J.K. "Medieval Descriptions of Cities." *Bulletin of the John Rylands Library* 48.2 (1966): 308-40.

Jones, R.O., ed. *A Literary History of Spain.* 8 vols. New York: Barnes & Noble, 1971.

Kubler, George. *Portuguese Plain Architecture: Between Spices and Diamonds, 1521-1708.* Middletown, CT: Wesleyan University Press, 1972.

Lisboa Quinhentista. Catalog of exhibit at Museu da Cidade, Lisbon. Ed. Irisalva Moita. Lisbon: Câmara Municipal, 1983.

Livermore, H.V. *A New History of Portugal.* New York: Cambridge University Press, 1976.

—. *The Origins of Spain and Portugal.* London: George Allen & Unwin, 1971.

Lynch, John. *Spain 1516-1598: From Nation State to World Empire.* Cambridge, MA: Basil Blackwell, 1992.

BIBLIOGRAPHY

MacKenney, Richard. *Sixteenth-Century Europe: Expansion and Conflict.* New York: St. Martin's Press, 1993.

Magalhães, Joaquim Romero. "As descrições geográficas de Lisboa: século 16." *Revista de História Económica e Social* 5 (January-June 1980): 15-54.

Markl, Dagoberto, and Fernando António Baptista Pereira. *O Renacimento.* Vol. 6 in *História da Arte em Portugal.* Lisbon: Alfa, 1986.

McAlister, Lyle N. *Spain & Portugal in the New World, 1492-1700.* Minneapolis: University of Minnesota Press, 1984.

Miskimin, Harry A., David Herlihy, and A. L. Udovitch, eds. *The Medieval City.* New Haven: Yale University Press, 1977.

Monter, William. *Frontiers of Heresy: The Spanish Inquisition from the Basque Lands to Sicily.* Cambridge and New York: Cambridge University Press, 1990.

Noreña, Carlos. *Juan Luis Vives.* The Hague: Martinus Nijhoff, 1970.

O'Malley, John W., SJ. *The First Jesuits.* Cambridge and London: Harvard University Press, 1993.

Pereira Bastos, Fernando. *Apontamentos sobre o Manuelino no Distrito de Lisboa.* Lisbon: Imprensa Nacional, Casa da Moeda, 1990.

Porfírio, José Luis. *Pintura Portuguesa/Portuguese Painting: Museu Nacional de Arte Antiga.* Lisbon: Quetzal, 1991.

Proença, Raúl, and Dionísio Sant'anna, eds. *Guia de Portugal.* Vol. 1. *Generalidades: Lisboa e Arredores.* 2d. ed. Lisbon: Fundação Calouste Gulbenkian, 1983.

Robertson, Ian. *Portugal: Blue Guide.* New York: Norton, 1988.

Roteiros de Arqueologia Portuguesa 1. Lisbon: Instituto Português do Património Cultural, 1986.

Rudolf Pfeiffer. *History of Classical Scholarship, 1300-1850.* Oxford: Clarendon Press, 1976.

Russel-Wood, A.J.R. *A World on the Move: The Portuguese in Africa, Asia and America, 1415-1808.* New York: St. Martin's Press, 1993.

Santana, Francisco, and Eduardo Sucena. *Dicionário da História de Lisboa.* Lisbon: Carlos Quintas e Asociados, 1994.

Santos, Piedade B., Teresa Rodrigues and Margarida Nogueira. *Lisboa Setecentista Vista por Estrangeiros.* Lisbon: Livros Horizonte, 1987.

Saraiva, António José, and Oscar Lopes. *História da literatura portuguesa.* Lisbon: Publicações Europa-América, 1980.

Saunders, A.C. de C.M. "The Life and Humor of João de Sá Panasco, o Negro, Former Slave, Court Jester and Gentleman of the Portuguese Royal Household (fl. 1524-1567)." In *Medieval and*

Renaissance Studies on Spain and Portugal in Honour of P.E. Russell. Ed. F.W. Hodcroft, D.G. Pattison, et al. Oxford: Society for the Study of Medieval Languages and Literatures, 1981, 180-91.

Serrão, Joel. *Cronologia da história de Portugal.* 4th ed. Lisbon: Livros Horizonte, 1980.

Stokes, I.N. Phelps. *The Iconography of Manhattan, 1498-1909.* Vol. 1. New York: Robert H. Dodd, 1915.

Tavares Diaz, Marina. *Lisboa Desaparecida.* Lisbon: Quimera, 1992.

Teyssier, P. "Lisbonne vue par un humaniste: l'*Urbis Olisiponis Descriptio* de Damião de Góis (1554)." In *Les Cités au temps de la Renaissance.* Ed. M.T. Jones-Davies. Paris: Université de Paris-Sorbonne, 1977, 137-51.

Tobriner, Marian Leona, SNJN. *Vives' Introduction to Wisdom: A Renaissance Textbook.* New York: Columbia University-Teacher's College Press, 1968.

Tyerman, Christopher. *England and the Crusades.* Chicago: University of Chicago Press, 1988.

Vásquez Cuesta, Pilar. *A lengua e a cultura portuguesas no tempo dos Filipes.* Lisbon: Publicações Europa América, 1988.

Watt, Tessa. *Cheap Print and Popular Piety, 1550-1640.* Cambridge and New York: Cambridge University Press, 1994.

Wheeler, Doulgas L. *Historical Dictionary of Portugal.* Metuchen, NJ: Scarecrow Press, 1993.

Wilkinson-Zerner, Catherine. *Juan de Herrera, Architect to Philip II of Spain.* New Haven: Yale University Press, 1993.

Wilcox, Donald J. *In Search of God and Self: Renaissance and Reformation Thought.* Boston: Houghton-Mifflin, 1975.

Wohl, Helmutt. "Recent Studies in Portuguese Post-Medieval Architecture." *Journal of the Society of Architectural Historians* 34.1 (1975): 67-73.

Woodward, William H. *Studies in Education during the Age of the Renaissance, 1400-1600.* New York: Columbia University Press, 1967, 180-210.

Wright, David, and Patrick Swift. *Lisbon: A Portrait and Guide.* New York: Scribners, 1971.

Wright, John Kirtland. *The Geographical Lore of the Time of the Crusades.* New York: Dover, 1965.

INDEX

INDEX

INDEX

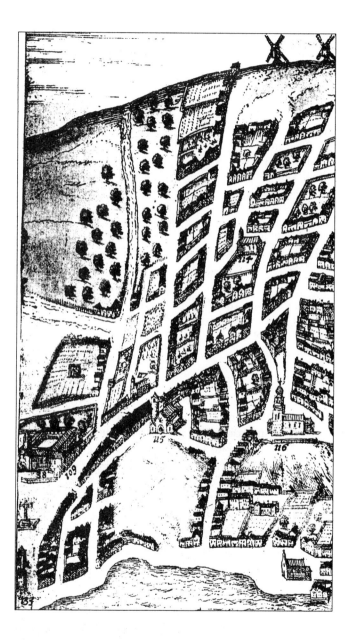

This Book Was Completed on June 30, 1996
At Italica Press, New York, NY. It Was
Set in Adobe Palatino, Monotype
Columbus Ornaments, and
Adobe Charlemagne. It
Was Printed on 50-lb
Natural Paper by
The Country Press
Middleborough,
Massachusetts
U. S. A.
* *
*